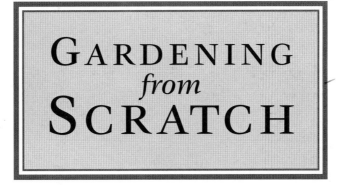

GARDENING
from
SCRATCH

Gay Search

GARDENING
from
SCRATCH

Photographs by
Jonathan Buckley

BBC Books

This book was published to
accompany the television series
entitled *Gardening from Scratch* which
was produced for BBC Television by
Catalyst Television

BBC Books,
a division of BBC Worldwide Limited,
Woodlands, 80 Wood Lane
London W12 0TT

Edited and designed for BBC Books by
Brown Packaging Ltd

Printed and bound in Great Britain by
Butler & Tanner Ltd,
Frome and London

Colour separation by
Radstock Reproductions Ltd,
Midsomer Norton

Cover printed by
Richard Clays Ltd, St Ives plc

Contents

INTRODUCTION

Are you one of the millions of people in this country who have a garden – whether it's a little concrete yard or something a bit bigger with grass and a few plants – but who don't think of themselves as gardeners?

Do you think that gardening is:

a) very difficult
b) too much like hard work
c) incontrovertible proof that middle age has set in?

Do you look out of your window on to a wilderness or urban desolation in miniature and think you'd love to do something with it so that you could actually enjoy using the space – but just don't know where to start?

If the answer to all of these questions – and particularly the last one – is 'yes', then this is the book that can change your life. Well, that is perhaps a slight exaggeration, but what we are setting out to show here is, first, that gardening, with the objective of creating an attractive and pleasurable space in which to relax, is hugely enjoyable, second, that you do not need an enormous amount of horticultural knowledge to make a successful start, and third, while it would be dishonest to suggest that there is no hard work involved, the rewards are so great that, as with so many other things, it ceases to feel like work.

What we're aiming to do is give you just enough basic and relevant knowledge to get you started, to help you make the best of your plot and keep it looking good – without overwhelming you with complex techniques or list upon list of plants that will make choice impossible. We are not assuming that gardening is going to become your major hobby and take up all your free time – though I suppose it's only fair to warn you that this could happen, as it's highly addictive, this gardening lark! This book is your starting point. It does not attempt to be comprehensive and there are lots of excellent books around to take you on to the next stage.

We won't, for instance, be covering greenhouses or rock gardens, though we will show easy ways to grow lovely colourful rock plants on flat ground. Similarly, while we won't deal in detail with growing vegetables, we will be showing you how to grow a range of easy vegetables – runner beans, lettuces, tomatoes – in containers because one of the most disproportionately satisfying rewards for beginner gardeners is being able to eat and enjoy the fruits – and veg – of their labours.

Creating an attractive garden is not just about horticulture, though, just as creating an attractive home is not just about DIY. In both instances, design is a key element.

Above and left: The transformation in our Square garden, which happened over just five months, is so dramatic that if it wasn't for the shed and the gate, it would be hard to believe it's the same plot. Seen from above, it's clear how successfully the triangular patio, the elliptical lawn and the curved sweep of gravel, replacing the narrow path of concrete slabs, have disguised the square shape and made the garden feel larger.

Garden Design

In its broadest sense, garden design covers everything from the layout (the shape of the patio, the paths and the lawn) to the choice of accessories (pots and furniture), the use of colour and, of course, the plants themselves. While many traditional gardeners still equate 'design' – usually said with a disdainful curl of the lip – with bricks and mortar, in fact the decision to plant silvery, purple-flowered lavender under pink roses, or a spiky grass in front of round-leafed bergenias is all about 'design', rather than horticulture.

What we are offering are some very simple, cheap design ideas which are, on the whole, easy to put into practice. Changing the shape of a lawn and therefore of the planting areas, for example, can make a dramatic difference to the look of the garden without costing you a penny. If the garden is the traditional oblong, then sweeping it across in a broad curve emphasizes the width, not the length, and makes it feel broader. In the process, you create borders of different shapes and dimensions, which also distract the eye from the rather boring shape and allow you to plant larger, more interesting groups of shrubs and perennials than you could have planted in the old straight-and-narrow borders down each side. A circular or oval lawn in a square garden does a similar job, creating deep planting areas in the corners and, by creating a strong central shape, makes the garden feel airy and spacious.

Changing the shape of a patio is another easy way of changing the layout of the garden at a stroke. In our Square garden, for example, we created a roughly triangular patio with the apex pointing out into the garden. It is not only more interesting visually, since you will have divided the rest of the garden up into unusual shapes, it's practical, too. Where space is limited, it gives plenty of room to put a table and chairs, whereas a conventional oblong patio of the same depth would have covered half the garden in paving.

The most interesting gardens are those that contain an element of surprise; those in which you don't see everything at once. In a small space it's not easy to achieve this, but it's not impossible. In our City garden, for instance, the tall planting in the main bed half way down obscures the view from the French windows, so that the seating area under the pergola isn't immediately visible – and so you are tempted out into the garden to explore. The tall planting also has the practical function of hiding the gas barbecue – not a pretty sight, but essential for getting maximum use and enjoyment out of the garden.

Focal points are also important in a garden, drawing the eye to where you want it to look and, just as important, away from where you don't. Many modern gardens are square at best or even wider than they are long and so, with nothing to distract it, the eye whizzes straight to the back fence and registers how close it is. Establishing something visually interesting in the centre of the garden or in the foreground – a group of pots, for instance – distracts the eye from the shallow nature of your plot. Alternatively, by putting a focal point in one corner, you draw the eye along the longest axis, the diagonal, which again, adds to the feeling of space. In our Square garden, we did this by using a spiky gold and green variegated phormium in a large pot. In our Oblong garden, we recycled the old summerhouse by swinging it round, out into the garden so that you could see its most attractive side – the front – from the house, reshaping the lawn to lead your eye to it, staining it a soft moss green and planting a lovely peachy-pink rose, 'Compassion' to climb over it. A seat, a sundial, an empty pot, or a particularly striking tree or shrub can be just as effective. But you can have too much of a good thing – too many focal points confuse the eye. So in a small space, keep it simple.

Your garden should be a haven, a retreat from the world, especially in cities where we live cheek by jowl with our neighbours. One very easy way to create a sense of privacy when you are overlooked is to put a roof over your head – a simple wooden pergola would do it, or even a ready-made rose arch, in each case covered with climbing plants. Although it may sound contradictory, this can also make the garden feel more spacious because it takes your eye up and out of the garden to the wider sky. Water has a similar effect, drawing the eye down and, without being too fanciful about it, into infinity – even though in reality it is only a shallow pond.

Colour is a tremendously important element in making an attractive garden – creating not merely moods, but optical illusions as well. In a small space, a few colours are far more effective than the whole spectrum used in close conjunction, where primary colours can cancel each other out. Pale colours recede and so, planted at the bottom of the garden, they seem further away than they actually are and make a space seem larger. Bright colours foreshorten so if you plant them at the bottom of the garden they will have the opposite effect. Don't be afraid to experiment with colour, though. It's often the combinations that shouldn't work in theory that are the most memorable and, if it really doesn't work – which means if *you* don't like it – then you can simply move one of the culprits.

If gardening is an art in four dimensions, the one that most new gardeners find hardest to cope with is time. In this age of instant everything, you don't want to plant up your garden and then wait five years to see a result. But you don't have to. While you will have to wait for trees and most shrubs to reach maturity, you can fill in with temporary eyecatchers like the spectacular thistle-like cardoon which will grow 2m (6ft 7in) in just a few months and then die down. Some grasses will grow almost as tall, and there are some easy annuals, sown directly into the soil, that will give you drama and colour for most of the summer – fashionable sunflowers or stunning annual climbers like morning glory, bought as young plants or seeds from the garden centre, that will cover an arch in one season.

What we want to do above all else is inspire you and give you the confidence to have a go. If you follow a few simple guidelines and let your imagination run free, you can create a garden that will give you more pleasure than you would have thought possible.

In the television series which this book accompanies, Helen Yemm, who has a wealth of experience in teaching gardening to beginners, takes the owners of three gardens through the basics. Our gardeners are all young, in their late twenties or early thirties, and all novices and we follow their progress as they transform their gardens with Helen's help.

STUART and MAL both work full-time and are both keen on a range of sports, so the time they have available for gardening is limited.

MARTIN runs his own business from home and SUSAN looks after Mary (18 months) with another baby due soon.

CATHERINE is married, with a toddler, Ben, and new baby Sophie, but her husband works long hours, so she is effectively a single-handed gardener.

Their gardens are typical of the small plots many new gardeners have to tackle and share many of the most common problems.

SQUARE GARDEN
Stuart and Mal's is small – less than 9 square metres (30sq ft), the sort of garden to be found on many housing estates built in the sixties. It was mainly grass, with a narrow concrete patio outside the sliding doors, a path to the back gate, narrow borders with some overgrown shrubs and a shed.

OBLONG GARDEN
Martin and Susan's is larger – about 18 x 6m (60 x 20ft) – the bog-standard suburban oblong with the bottom third fenced off as a vegetable garden. Again, there were narrow beds down the sides and – thanks in part to two large dogs – a rectangle of very scrubby lawn.

CITY GARDEN
Catherine's garden is a small city backyard, less than 9 x 6m (30 x 20ft) behind a terraced Victorian house. There are brick walls on one side and along the bottom with a new fence topped by trellis on the other side. Before we got to work on it, the central area was more mud than grass, with a few neglected roses and a few equally neglected climbers and shrubs in the borders.

The very first thing to do when you acquire a garden is to take a good look at it and ask some basic questions. Which way does it face, for example? It's important to know this because it will dictate the amount of sun and shade in your garden and where it falls at different times of day. That in turn affects your choice of plants and where you should site sitting-out areas – and, yes, you should think about more than one sitting area to include the barbecue and so on.

Don't worry if you haven't used a compass since cubs or brownies – working out the direction is quite simple. If the early morning sun streams in through your back windows but is off the garden by mid to late afternoon, this means it faces east. If it faces west, you will get the sun from midday until it sets. North-facing gardens will get a reasonable amount of sun in midsummer, but will be largely in shade when the sun is lower in the sky – in autumn, winter and spring. If your garden faces south you will get sun in the garden pretty well all day.

You might think the sunniest spot is the obvious place for seating or eating areas – and certainly you'll want to make the most of early morning sun for breakfast in the garden, and the evening sun for supper. But would you really want to have lunch in the midday sun? Think about another, shadier, spot or about creating your own shade as they do in Mediterranean countries with a pergola draped in climbers.

The next thing you'll need to know is what kind of soil you have because this dictates what will grow most easily and successfully. It really isn't worth battling against nature. With a headstart of several billion years, she always wins. While I know

Above: Our City garden at night. Even a very simple DIY lighting system like the one we installed allows you to get maximum benefit from the garden. On warm summer evenings it transforms the garden into a valuable outside room and, on cold winter nights, it means you can enjoy the look of it, too.

Right: The temptation in very small gardens is often to keep the borders narrow and the plants in them very small, to make the space feel larger. But, as this wide bed in our City garden proves, it is generous planting areas and very tall plants, such as this thistle-like cardoon on the right and the striped grass, which divide up the garden and create an illusion of space.

that checking out soil doesn't rank at the top of the all-time excitement list, it really is half an hour extremely well spent. If you don't know, for example, that your soil is limy, then shrubs like rhododendrons and camellias will just sicken and die because they must have an acid soil. We'll go into all that in more detail later.

Finally, you need to take stock, have a look at what's already in the garden, what is lovely, what might be worth keeping with a bit of a sort-out and what will definitely have to go. In an ideal world, you should leave the garden for a whole year to see what comes up but, if it really is a tip and you're bubbling over with enthusiasm to get stuck in, that approach doesn't make sense. If you've only just moved in, you could ask the previous occupiers what's there. If you've been there some time, then you'll have some idea of what flowers there are, what colour they are and whether you like them. If you really don't have a clue about what you've got in the garden, then ask a man (or woman) who does. This is where relatives, colleagues or neighbours can be worth their weight in gold – there's bound to be one keen gardener among them.

Get your gardening friend to walk round the garden with you to identify the plants. Take a notebook, a packet of plastic plant labels, an indelible marker and some garden string. Write down each name as you go, both on a rough sketch plan in your notebook and on a label, with as much additional information as you can squeeze on – 'tall evergreen', for instance, or 'pale pink flowers in May' – and tie it to the tree or shrub with string. Once you've made them a cup of tea or poured them a stiff drink, they will probably be happy to give you more information about the plants in your garden – what needs doing to them and what their habits are. 'Cut back to 15cm (6in) from the ground in early spring' is a useful tip, as is 'inclined to sprawl, so provide support'.

Armed with your notebook, visit the library or invest in a good illustrated encyclopaedia of plants to see what your plants look like at their best. Once you know what you've got and what it does, you're then much better able to decide whether to keep it. A word of advice – even if there is nothing in the garden you really want to keep, think very hard before you rip everything out. A few mature plants give you the structure that newly planted gardens lack. They also give you privacy – something you may not appreciate until it's too late – so hang on to a few shrubs or trees for a couple more years.

You and your garden

Once you've got a picture of the garden, you need to ask yourself a few questions. What, primarily, do you want the garden for? Are you going to use it mostly for sitting in after work and at weekends, and for entertaining friends? If that's the case, do you really need a lawn? Lawns need cutting regularly and, though it doesn't take long, it's surprising how difficult it can be to find the time. And time, of course, is another key question – how many hours are you prepared to spend on the garden each week? If it's not very many, then you need to plan for low maintenance right from the start. Many new gardeners think that putting the whole area down to grass is a low-maintenance option, but of course it isn't. If a lawn is to look halfway decent, it will need cutting regularly – not to mention feeding and weeding and watering. Much better to choose a combination of low-maintenance plants and hard landscaping – slabs, brick or, cheapest of all and easiest to lay, gravel – and devote what time you have to looking after the plants.

If you are out all day, then plan your garden with the evening in mind – put the seating area where you catch the last of the sun, choose plants that look good in fading light – mainly pale pinks, yellows and whites – and, of course, plants which are most strongly scented at night. After all, you tailor your home to suit your tastes and your lifestyle, so why not do the same with your garden?

Basic kit

As a stroll through the tool department of any garden centre will quickly reveal, there is a bewildering array of tackle on sale, much of it brightly coloured, shiny and designed to appeal to gadget-lovers. There are, however, only a few tools you will actually need to get you started.

If you are on a really tight budget, try to track down some second-hand, good-quality tools, rather than buying cheap new ones. Look in local papers or publications like *Exchange & Mart*. Try junk shops or car boot sales – though I'm slightly uneasy about recommending the latter because, as the police will tell you, a lot of the stuff for sale there was stolen from someone's shed the night before.

The following tools are all illustrated on pages 14–15, with keys to the photographs on page 16.

The must haves

SPADE (2)

The essential tool for digging over, making holes for planting and so on. As with all tools, buy the best quality you can afford. Stainless steel is superb, will last you a lifetime and makes digging easier because it slides through the soil. But it is very expensive. If you can't afford it, buy one made from forged steel (not pressed steel) by a reputable firm. Although the average British gardener is now a good few inches taller than their grandparents were, the spade manufacturers have only just begun to catch on to this fact. Some are now producing spades with shafts of different lengths. Choosing a spade of the right length for you can prevent backache. If you're a woman or an average-sized man, a border spade which has a slightly smaller blade might be a better bet.

FORK (1)

Useful for making an impression on very heavy or hard-baked ground. The same rule applies to buying forks as to spades, except that forged steel is good enough. If you can afford only one of the two, some very good gardeners of my acquaintance would choose a fork, because it can double as a spade and a rake. I personally would go for a spade because there are jobs it can do that a fork can't, or not as easily. Digging planting holes in sandy soil with a fork is both time-consuming and frustrating.

TROWEL (16) AND HAND FORK (11)

Invaluable for making small planting holes and, if you can't afford a hand fork right away, a trowel can be used for weeding, too. Given that it's relatively easy to mislay hand trowels in the vegetation, stainless steel is an extravagance, so go for forged steel from a reputable firm instead. You would be astonished at how easy it is to bend a very cheap one into total uselessness.

SECATEURS (14)

Sharp secateurs, whether the anvil or the parrot-bill type, are essential for pruning. The emphasis is on 'sharp'. Allowed to become blunt, they become very hard work to use, and tear the stems you're pruning rather than cutting them, which in turn damages the plants. Buy the best you can afford, keep them clean and oiled and get them sharpened every year. And don't under any circumstances use them to cut wire!

GARDEN KNIFE (15)

Knives are invaluable for a whole range of jobs in the garden – from opening plastic bags of compost to cutting garden twine, from cutting sweet peas for the house to light pruning. (Yes, I know some gardeners use their secateurs for all of these cutting jobs, but that makes them blunter more quickly and garden knives are quite cheap to buy anyway.) Look for a simple, single-bladed pocket knife. I used to choose tasteful gardening colours like green and brown but, having had several knives blend so perfectly with their surroundings that I couldn't find them amongst the greenery, I now have a bright red knife instead which is very much more difficult to lose!

HOSE (6)

Adequate watering is essential. In a hot dry spell, not even the most dedicated beginner is going to give newly planted trees and shrubs the amount of water they need with a watering-can. You can buy cheap 'hoseboxes' now, with enough hose for a small garden, neatly contained in a small, easily-stored, light plastic housing. Get a basic, adjustable nozzle for it and a very simple sprinkler.

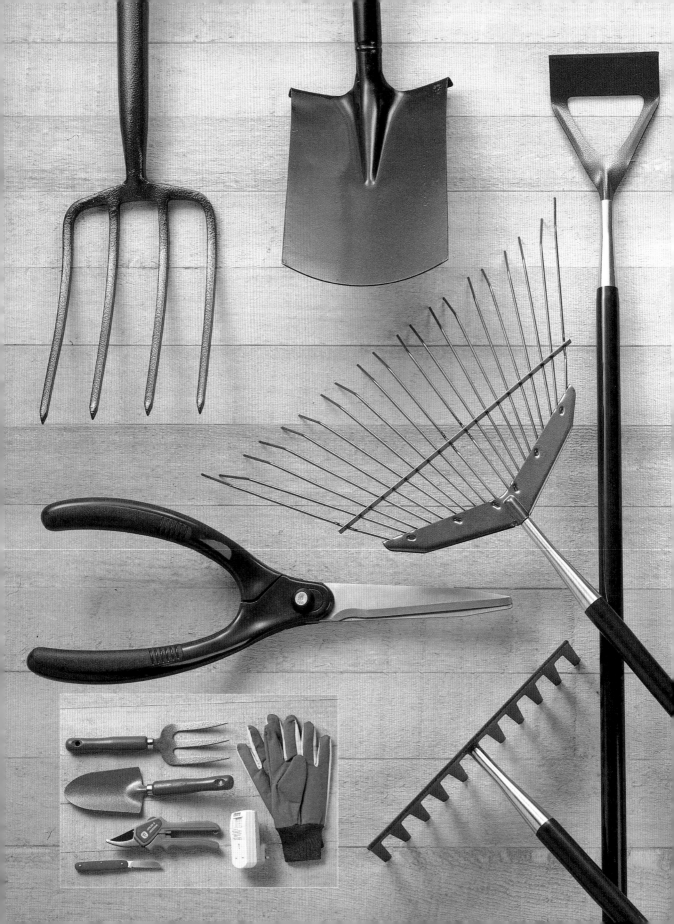

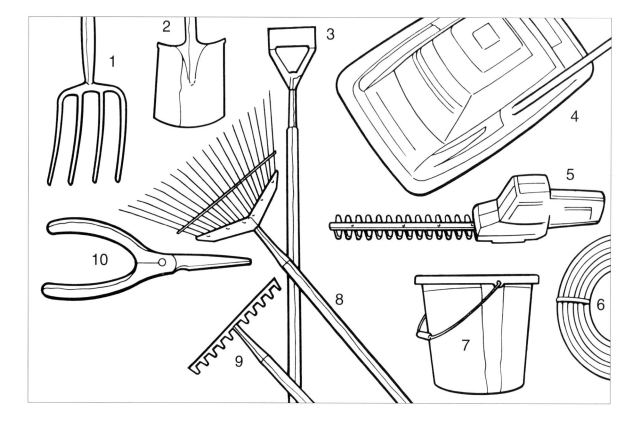

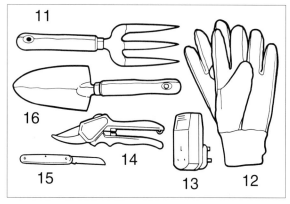

BUCKET (7)

A stout plastic bucket will serve a multitude of purposes – a mini wheelbarrow to hold the weeds or to transport quantities of compost, bark and so on, a watering can when you don't need to be too careful, a reservoir in which to soak plants in their pots prior to planting out – the list is endless.

LAWN MOWER (4)

If you have a lawn, you must have a lawn mower or invest in a goat. The ordinary push mower in theory is ideal for a small garden and a young, fit gardener but, in fact, they are more expensive than the basic electric ones. Hover mowers, with rotary blades, are fine for workaday lawns, but cylinder mowers with a number of rotating blades cut the grass like a series of pairs of scissors to give a finer finish. If you can afford it, buy a mower with a grass box which picks up the clippings to save you raking them up afterwards.

CIRCUIT BREAKER (13)

When you buy your first electric powered tool, you must also buy a circuit breaker (or Residual Current Device – RCD) if your house is more than a few years old and one hasn't been built in. They are quite expensive but can save your life – should you be unlucky enough to slice through the cable, they will shut off the power instantly, so there is no danger of electrocution.

Optional tools

RAKE (9)
Invaluable for levelling soil in preparation for sowing seed, but only worth buying if you're going to be doing this on a regular basis – if you're planning to grow vegetables or lots of annuals, for instance. If you think you are only going to need a rake initially – levelling the soil to lay a lawn, for example, or after you've dug over beds in preparation for permanent planting – then borrow or hire one.

SPRING-TINED RAKE (8)
This has a fan of fine metal teeth and is used for raking the thatch (dead grass, moss and so on) out of a lawn in the spring (hence its misnomer, the spring-time rake), raking up grass clippings if your mower doesn't collect them, or leaves in the autumn. If you have a lawn, then you will definitely need one of these.

HOE (3)
The Dutch hoe is useful for weeding beds and borders, though not essential in a small garden. If you don't mind a bit of bending, you can do the job as efficiently with a hand fork – which, of course, gets you closer to your plants.

These last three tools are also available as snap-on heads, so that you can buy just one shaft and fix on the appropriate business end as you need it. It's cheaper and saves on storage space as well.

SHEARS (10)
If you have hedges you will need shears to keep them trimmed but, if you only trim them once or twice a year, you can easily borrow or hire a pair.

ELECTRIC HEDGE TRIMMERS (5)
These make short work of hedge trimming so, if you have a lot of hedges to deal with, they are worth buying. You can now buy cordless, rechargeable hedge trimmers which are safer to use and cut for about an hour and a half on one charge. Wear eye protection to prevent any bits of flying twig from damaging your eyes.

GARDENING GLOVES (12)
It is always a good idea to wear gloves if you are handling soil that might have been fouled by dogs or cats and if you live in a town, there's very little chance of escaping the latter. Wear them, too, when you're handling chemicals and fertilizers.

Taking care

Having spent a lot of money on tools, it makes sense to take care of them. Try and clean them each time you use them. It only takes a couple of minutes to keep them in good condition, and it's hard work, trying to dig with a spade pitted with rust and blunted by caked-on mud. Sluice them down with the hose or use a piece of wood to scrape the mud off, dry them thoroughly and wipe them with an oily rag. Do the same with the cutting tools and get them professionally sharpened every season, though you can keep your garden knife sharp with a grinding stone. The best time to get cutting tools sharpened is mid/late winter. Wait until the first nice weekend of spring and you'll find everyone else has had the same idea.

Look after yourself as well. Learn to pace yourself in the garden. Nothing will dampen enthusiasm faster than going at it flat out and finding yourself aching in places you didn't even know you had. Wear sensible, comfortable old clothes – long trousers tend to be better than shorts if you're mowing or strimming, because flying stones and even flying grass can cause tiny cuts and rashes. Don't wear flip-flops or plimsolls, especially for digging or mowing. Casualty departments still see too many people with foot injuries from gardening in silly shoes. Wear stout boots or shoes. Steel-capped Doc Martens are perfect – and cool.

If you don't have a current tetanus vaccination, get it done. It takes seconds, and lasts five years.

It's just common sense really, and the most important thing to remember is – it's fun!

WALLS, FENCES AND CLIMBERS

Above: If pegged down on to the soil, ivy will first produce roots and then put out shoots at every leaf joint along the stem. This new growth will climb the wall or fence, clinging on as it goes and will give you a much broader and better coverage in a shorter time.

Left: For scramblers like the golden hop, clematis or solanum, the quickest and easiest method of support on a fence is to use pieces of wide-gauge sheep netting stapled on to the posts.

Above: Smaller-gauge chicken wire is an effective support for scramblers on a post or drainpipe.

Right: Tensioned wire is a good support for wall shrubs and climbing roses.

The boundaries of your garden are extremely important. They give you privacy and keep out unwanted visitors – canine, feral or human! Nothing is less conducive to a comfortable and relaxed garden than the feeling that you are over-looked. And where space is limited, they also offer the chance to bring more colour and scent into the garden in the form of lovely climbing plants. But first you must assess the state of the boundaries.

In the Square garden, the fences needed some repairs. Most of the damage – the odd broken trellis panel on top of the fences, missing battens, a few broken planks and one missing panel – was relatively easily rectified, and the rest was in good enough condition to last four or five more years. We found a couple of second-hand fencing panels in a skip. The better of the two replaced the missing panel and the other was cannibalized for repairs. With a few new panels of squared trellis, the job was done very cheaply.

The only remaining problem was that the repaired fences looked like a brindled cat, in various shades of brown. We stained it all a uniform dark brown with a plant-friendly wood stain (creosote is not friendly to plants). This is a good neutral colour which blends into the background and makes a good foil for plants.

In our Oblong garden, the fences ranged from the tolerably good to the almost non-existent. On the north-east facing side, the fence was in a

reasonably good condition, so it seemed an extravagance to replace it at this stage. In fact, the next door neighbour, wanting more privacy, chose to put up some 1.8m (6ft) fences later that summer.

On the south-west facing side, however, the fence was in a terrible state, with some panels down, others leaning at a crazy angle and some so badly damaged that there were more gaps than fencing. The reason for this state of affairs is that this is the side that gets the full force of the prevailing south-westerly winds. The problem is that, being on top of a hill, this is a very windy garden. There was no alternative but to replace all the panels, for which we needed the agreement of the neighbours on this side, since technically the fence was their responsibility. You must always check which of your boundary fences is your responsibility since, in most instances, only one of them will be. Usually it is the fence with the posts on your side that belongs to you. Any fence along the bottom of the garden will probably be a responsibility shared between you and the house backing on to you.

To counteract the strength of the wind, we used stouter posts than before – 10 x 10cm (4 x 4in) rather than 7.5 x 7.5cm (3 x 3in) – with 1.5m (5ft) high panels and 30cm (1ft) of trellis on the top. The trellis not only allows the wind to filter through but, being open, it's not as claustrophobic as solid panels would have been.

One alternative where a new boundary is essential but money is tight is to use stout, squared trellis panels as fencing and grow climbing plants over

---

Six good climbers/ wall shrubs for shade

Ivy (*hedera*)

Virginia creeper (*Parthenocissus quinquefolia*)

Climbing hydrangea (*Hydrangea petiolaris*)

Clematis (*C. montana* and some hybrids like 'Nellie Moser' and 'Carnaby')

Roses ('Golden Showers', 'Madame Alfred Carriere', 'Danse de Feu')

Firethorn (*pyracantha*)

For sun

Passion flower (*passiflora*)

Roses (most)

Summer-flowering jasmine (*Jasminum officinale*)

Clematis

Wisteria

Honeysuckle (*lonicera*)

---

them – ideally mostly evergreens so you have cover in winter. It will take a couple of years before the panels are more or less covered by the plants, though in the meantime annual climbers like sweet peas (*Lathyrus odoratus*), morning glories (*ipomoea*), or even runner beans with their glorious scarlet flowers, give colour while the more permanent plants are getting established.

Once the new fences were up, their aggressive ginger colour was rather dominant. They do weather down to a more acceptable grey-brown colour within a year or two, but we decided to stain them, again with a dark brown, plant-friendly wood stain.

In the City garden, there was a fairly new fence along the south-facing side made from 1.5m (5ft) panels with 30cm (1ft) of trellis on top. This time we stained it with a very thin, creamy-white stain which produced an almost lime-washed look to give a light, neutral background for the plants.

The other boundaries in this garden were brick walls, obviously built at different times. The one at the bottom of the garden was probably built at the same time as the house and was of dark, almost sooty bricks. The other wall was more recent, made of second-hand bricks, some of which had probably once been part of a swimming baths since they still had a thick crust of turquoise paint. As the bricks were all different, and not particularly attractive in their raw state, we decided to paint them with masonry paint. A dark, shady yard immediately becomes much lighter and brighter with a coat of white or pastel paint.

The choice of colour plays an important part in the effect you want to create. White is an excellent choice if you want a Mediterranean feel, with lots of spiky plants and strong, hot colours – brilliant scarlet geraniums, for instance, would look superb in this setting. It really looks at its best in bright sunshine, though, and can look a bit stark and cold on dull days. Other pastel shades create different effects – very pale yellow, beige or peach lighten the area just as effectively, but are warmer than white. Alternatively, if you're feeling brave go for a Provençal or Tuscan look with deeper shades of ochre or terracotta, washed over with a very thin coat of white emulsion to give it an authentic sun-bleached look.

We chose a buttery yellow to bring a feeling of sunshine into the garden even in the depths of winter. It is also a very good foil for blue and white flowers and the smoky blue-green wood stain we were to use for the trellis panels on the walls, the woodwork of the new pergola and the garden furniture. Woodstains are wonderful for transforming garden features at reasonably low cost. They now come in a wide range of colours – everything from the subtle, pale mossy green we used to transform the old shed in the Oblong garden to strong reds and yellows. Obviously colours must be chosen with care to fit in with the style of the garden. Bright primary colours, for example, will probably work best in a modern, unashamedly urban garden, while more subtle shades will work better in more traditional surroundings and with a more cottagey style of planting.

If you have chain-link fencing as your boundary, you have got rather more of a problem. As it's usually only 1m (40in) or so high, it gives you no privacy and, while you can grow plants such as ivy or sweet peas over it, that still doesn't hide its utilitarian appearance. You could plant a hedge in front, but that will take several years to grow and requires regular clipping. Hedges are greedy feeders, too, so it means you can't grow anything else

close to it – not ideal in a small garden. Your best bet is simply to replace it with wooden posts and panels as soon as your finances allow.

Training climbers

Having got your boundaries sorted out, you can then decide how best to make use of them. In the City garden, there were already a number of climbers which between them provided a comprehensive catalogue of how not to support climbers! There was a honeysuckle, about five years old but still twined round the original cane from the garden centre. Its green plastic ties were still in position and the crowded stems had grown into a woody spiral. There were climbers with no supports and others that were tied on to the trellis with bits of torn-up shirt.

> *Always tie wall shrubs to the support and don't push young stems behind it*

Climbers need to be grown against strong supports. From an aesthetic point of view, the supports themselves should be either virtually invisible or, alternatively, extremely visible – making them attractive features in their own right. If you want to use trellis, for instance, use it in a decorative way. In the City garden, we cut down 1.8 x 1.2m (6 x 4ft) squared trellis panels to 1.2 x 1.2m (4 x 4ft), stained them an attractive colour and fixed them as diamonds on the wall, creating a strong architectural effect. Another excellent way of using a support as a focal point is a simple wigwam or obelisk made from stained battens, with morning glory or sweet peas. Before you decide on a method of support, however, you need to know the type of climber you have. They fall into four basic categories.

THE SELF CLINGERS

This category includes ivy (*hedera*), Virginia creeper (*Parthenocissus quinquefolia*) and the climbing hydrangea (*H. petiolaris*) and these plants all produce little clumps of aerial roots that cling on to the wall or fence by themselves. The plants will need a

Above and below: Merely giving the fences a fashionable limed
look with white wood stain and painting the grimy brick walls
a warm, sunny yellow makes a huge difference to this garden.
Creating interest in the corners – the pergola on the left and the
curved planting area on the right – has made the space feel
larger by drawing the eye along the diagonals, and has
eliminated its former, rather boxy feel.

Left: The deep blue clematis 'Lasurstern'.

Below: Clematis such as this small-flowered C.viticella 'Little Nell' are stunning climbers and aren't difficult to grow, provided you plant them correctly, 10–15cm (4–6in) deeper than they are in their pots, and water and feed them well.

bit of support until established, though, because it is only the new growth that clings – not the roots already on the stems.

You can just leave the plant on the cane and point it at the wall to let the plant find its own way. Alternatively, you can take it off its cane, spread the growths out and attach them to the wall with individual self-adhesive plant ties or even blobs of blu-tack. For wide and fast cover with ivy, spread one stem out along the soil at the base of the wall on each side and cover it with soil, just brushing it off the leaves themselves. In a few months, it will root and send up new growths from every rooted leaf joint.

Ivy and Virginia creeper have a reputation for damaging walls – largely undeserved if the pointing and the bricks are sound.

THE SCRAMBLERS

The scramblers include clematis, passion flower (*passiflora*) and sweet peas (*Lathyrus odoratus*) which cling on by means of small, curly tendrils that wrap themselves tightly around anything they come across. Solanum is another scrambler but it uses its leaves rather like elbows, hooking them on to any means of support.

There are various methods of supporting scramblers. On the front of a house, you need to create a wire grid. Attach stout horizontal wires about 45cm (18in) apart. Use hammer-in vine eyes if yours is an old house or, if it's more modern, wall plugs and screw-in eyes fixed in pre-drilled holes in the mortar. If there is a wide area to cover, use tension bolts, where the eye itself can be turned to give the

---

Six good roses

Bush rose

'Margaret Merrill' – Blush-white flowers with a sweet perfume all summer

Shrub rose

'Buff Beauty' – Apricot-buff flowers all summer

English rose

'Graham Stuart Thomas' – Clear yellow flowers all season

Patio rose

'The Fairy' – Small pink flowers from early summer to late autumn

Climber

'Compassion' – Peachy-apricot flowers all summer with glossy deep green leaves

Rambler

'Alberic Barbier' – Creamy-white flowers in midsummer with some later

---

wire the neccessary tension. Then, using finer wire, make a grid with vertical wires about 45cm (18in) apart. Wrap the end round the top wire, wrap it once round the intervening wires and then wrap it several times round the bottom wire in order to secure it firmly.

If you are growing scramblers on a fence, cover the panels with pieces of sheep netting (very like chicken wire only with much larger holes). Stretch the netting across and fix it to the fence posts on each side with five or six galvanized staples. It's a bit shiny when you first put it up, but it soon weathers down to a dull grey and becomes virtually invisible and, of course, the plants will soon cover it anyway. You can use it on walls as well, but in this case you would need lead-headed nails to hold it in place.

For pillars or pergolas, the easiest method of giving your climbers a ready support is to wrap a piece of chicken wire loosely round the post, using the cut ends of the wire bent back on themselves to hold it in place. Bend all the cut ends to the inside so none is sticking out and then there is no risk of anyone scratching themselves.

THE TWINERS

The twiners include flowers such as honeysuckle (*lonicera*), summer jasmine (*jasminum*), wisteria and foliage climbers such as golden hop (*humulus*). They all climb by twining their stems around a support. The best method for supporting them on a wall or fence is a grid of wires. The stem twines around the support so there must be room for the plant to go behind it. If the posts are on your side of the fence and stand proud of the panels, you can hold the wires in place with galvanized staples.

If you're putting wires on the other side of the fence (having first asked your neighbour's permission, of course!), it's a bit more tricky because the panels will be flush with the posts. In this case, you can either use screw-in vine eyes, which will stand proud, or you can nail a 5 x 5cm (2 x 2in) vertical batten down the post and fix the wires to it with staples.

If you are using staples, there's a very simple technique for getting enough tension on the wires. Hammer the staples almost home on all the posts and then cut a piece of wire to length, adding an extra 45cm (18in) or so. Fix the wire at one end, hammering the staple home, then thread it through the intervening staples. If the last staple is on a post in a corner, or flush up against a wall, stop at the last-but-one post. Wrap the free end of wire round a stout piece of wood, taking up most of the slack, and then put the end of the piece of wood against the side of the fence post or batten and strain the wire tight. While you're holding it, get a helper to hammer the staple home, then cut off most of the spare wire and wrap the remainder back on itself.

To finish off the last panel, fix the wire to the post in the corner (or up against the wall), partially hammer in a second staple on the last-but-one fence post, thread the wire through and, reversing the process, strain the wire against the post in the opposite direction.

Six good clematis

Small flowered

Clematis montana 'Tetrarose' – Deep pink flowers and bronze foliage from March to April

Clematis alpina 'Frances Rives' – Nodding blue and white flowers from March to April

Clematis viticella 'Etoile Violette' – Rich violet flowers from midsummer to autumn

Large flowered

C. 'Perle d'Azur' – Sky-blue flowers with bright green-gold stamens in the centre from mid to late summer

C. 'Marie Boisselot' – Large white flowers from June to July and again in late summer

Evergreen

Clematis armandii – Long slender leaves with white flowers from March to April. For a sheltered south- or west-facing wall

Wall shrubs

Wall shrubs have no means of supporting themselves and must be tied to some form of support. Horizontal wires are probably the best bet for most wall shrubs and climbing roses – they don't need vertical ones. Always tie the stems to the frame work, rather than tucking them behind the wires as they may become distorted as they grow, especially as they become woody.

The best material for ties is soft green garden twine. It will eventually decompose and – unlike plastic or wire – it will never cut into the plant. Tie it in a bow so that it's easy to undo.

Planting climbers

The most important point to remember about planting any climber or wall shrub is that you never plant too close to the walls, where the soil is usually very dry and poor. The wall often shields the plant from rain, as well as preventing its roots from spreading in every direction. The main stem of the climber should be at least 30cm (1ft) from the wall.

The one exception to this rule is clematis, which you should plant 10–15cm (4–6in) deeper than they are in their pots to avoid clematis wilt. As the disease stops at soil level, deep planting ensures there are healthy buds under the soil to produce new growth. If there is no new growth by late spring, dig out the rootball and replace it, perhaps with one of the small-flowered types, such as *C. viticella* or *C. texensis* which seem less prone to wilt.

DOWN TO EARTH

For many years now, in one way or another, I've been trying to pass on my passion for gardening to new gardeners and inspire them enough to have a go themselves. The one problem I still haven't cracked is how to deal with the subject of soil. Once people have got the gardening bug, they want to start planting colourful shrubs and perennials and watch them grow. They don't want to have to learn all about soil because it's boring. But there is no doubt at all that the most important element in growing plants successfully is good, fertile soil. Quite simply, if your soil is rubbish, you will never have a good garden – no matter how much work you put in, no matter how much money you spend. So, please, don't skip this chapter. I promise that everything in it is strictly relevant to you as a new gardener.

Acidity and alkalinity

You need to know two things about your soil. First, is it acid or alkaline, heavy and sticky or thin and sandy? And, second, how can you improve it so that your plants will thrive? The acidity or alkalinity of your soil – measured on a scale called pH – determines which plants you can grow successfully. Let's take rhododendrons and azaleas, those most eye catching of spring-flowering shrubs. They must have an acid soil because they hate lime and in an alkaline soil – one that contains lime – they will quickly sicken and die. As they're not cheap plants to buy, planting them in unsuitable soil is a waste of money as well as being extremely disheartening. Other acid-lovers include camellias, summer-flowering heathers – the winter ones will tolerate most soils – and pieris, a lovely evergreen shrub with vivid scarlet foliage in spring. The pH of your soil will also affect the colour of hydrangea flowers – on acid soils they are pink, on alkaline ones blue, and even if you buy a very popular variety called 'Blue Wave', unless yours is an acid soil, your 'wave' will be pink!

At any garden centre, you can buy a cheap, simple lime-testing kit that comes complete with test tubes and chemicals. There are more expensive

Above: If your soil is not acid enough for plants like this Japanese maple (Acer palmatum), grow them in containers in lime-free compost.

Above: Although it may seem like a chore, testing your soil will save you money and disappointment.

Right: Just four months after planting, the thriving striped miscanthus, feathery fennel and white cosmos are living proof that feeding the soil with organic matter and fertilizer pays dividends.

electronic soil-testing meters on the market but, as you'll use it only occasionally, it's better to borrow a kit like this than to buy.

How to test your soil

Take samples of soil from several parts of the garden because you might just hit a patch where, say, cement has been buried, giving a more alkaline reading than the rest of the garden. Dig down a little rather than taking it off the top because that's where it will affect the plants. While the colour of the liquid in the test tube is unlikely to be as vivid as those on the instructions, it should be quite clear what type of soil you've got.

Most plants – acid-lovers aside – will thrive in a soil that's neutral or close to it and there are very few, members of the cabbage family mainly, that won't grow well in an acid soil. If you have an alkaline soil and you're passionate about camellias, grow them in containers in lime-free – 'ericaceous' – compost.

Don't even attempt to alter the nature of your soil because, while it might work in the short term, it won't in the long run. And don't forget there are masses of lovely shrubs like mock orange (*philadelphus*), lilac (*syringa*), lavender (*lavendula*) and clematis that will thrive in alkaline soil.

Soil texture

The best way to determine the texture of your soil is, quite simply, to handle it.

CLAY AND SILT

If you can cut slices with a spade – and almost make pots with it – you've got heavy clay. If you can squeeze it into a ball in your hand and it feels silky to touch, then you've got silt. Both have similar problems. They get waterlogged and sticky in winter and dry out like concrete in summer. Not only does this make digging very hard work, plants don't like such extreme states as their roots are either drowning in water and can't get air, or they can't get enough water. Clay and silt soils are slow to warm up in spring, as well as being wet, so you can't sow seeds early. But they are usually the most fertile soils and you can improve them by digging in coarse grit or gravel and organic matter to open up the soil texture and improve aeration and drainage.

If you have a new border, the best way is to trench it. Dig a trench to one spade's depth, piling the soil to one side. Then break up the bottom of the trench with a fork (or a crowbar if the soil is really compacted) and mix in some organic matter and grit. Working backwards, start digging another trench behind the first, pushing the soil forwards into it. When it's half full, add more grit and organic matter so that you are working both in at several levels. Then complete digging the second trench and filling up the first. Carry on until you've dug out the final trench, then refill it with grit, organic matter and the soil from the first trench (see page 31).

> *Fertile soil is the key to growing plants successfully*

If you want to keep some of the plants in the border, it is slightly more difficult. The plants' roots extend as widely below the ground as the canopy of its branches above. So, within that area, simply spread grit and compost on top of the soil and fork it in very lightly. As for the rest of the border, work in grit and compost to one spade's depth.

SANDY AND CHALKY SOILS

If it's impossible to make a ball of soil in your hand no matter how hard you squeeze, and it feels gritty, then you've got a light, free-draining sandy soil. If it's greyish in colour and has small white lumps of chalk in it, then it's a chalky soil. These light, free-draining soils are much easier to work than clay and they warm up very quickly in spring. Their disadvantage is that they dry out too quickly in summer and nutrients are washed through the soil so fast that the plants don't benefit from them.

You need to make these soils more moisture retentive by digging in bulky organic matter to act like a sponge in the soil, holding in water and nutrients longer. Mulching – spreading a layer of organic matter, gravel or even black polythene on top of the soil to suppress weeds and keep moisture in – is a good idea with any soil, but especially useful here.

LOAM

This is the best sort of soil – easy to work and warming up quickly in spring, so that you can sow earlier than you could on heavier, colder soil. Loam is both moisture retentive and relatively free draining so that it neither gets waterlogged nor dries out too quickly.

Feeding the soil

The idea that soil needs feeding comes as a big surprise to many new gardeners. Soil in the wild, in fact, is always being fed with organic matter (something – whether animal or vegetable – which was once alive but is now dead). This rots down, working its way back into the soil and producing micro-organisms that provide nutrients for the plants. This happens in gardens, too, but to a much lesser extent and, of course, we garden far more intensively and expect to get a lot more out of our soil than nature does. This means you must feed your soil with organic matter and fertilizers.

ORGANIC MATTER

This comes in all sorts of different forms. Farmyard or stable manure is probably the one with which most new gardeners are familiar. It is an excellent soil improver *provided* it is well rotted – it should be dark and crumbly and shouldn't smell.

Garden compost, made from all the clippings and prunings from the garden, as well as vegetable waste from the kitchen, is a good source of organic matter. As a new gardener, though, you won't have any, and since compost bins or heaps take up valu-

able garden room, you may prefer to use all the available space for sowing plants and buy the comparatively small quantities of compost you'll need.

Leaf mould is another excellent, home-made soil conditioner, though you need lots of leaves and space in which to process them. There are other products you can buy at the garden centre – composted bark, composted straw, products based on cow manure, spent mushroom compost (though do get the de-limed sort if you can, especially if you have a neutral or acid soil), spent hops, cocoa shells (which smell of chocolate and are slightly acidic). There are also concentrated manure products available which are very good for feeding the soil, but not bulky enough to make it more moisture retentive or less sticky. Where that is the aim, it's best to go for a bulkier product.

FERTILIZERS

There is a bewildering array of fertilizers available at the garden centre. They break down into two main types – organic, like the gruesome-sounding blood, fish and bone or pelletted chicken manure, and the inorganic, such as sulphate of potash, rose fertilizer or growmore (not a brand name, but a formula) which are manufactured. Plants can't tell the difference between organic and inorganic, but green gardeners prefer the organic kinds because inorganics can leech through the soil into the water supply. Organic and inorganic are then further sub-divided into quick-release and slow-release fertilizers. The former, like dried blood and sulphate of ammonia, give plants a rapid boost while the latter, such as hoof and horn and rock potash, will take several months to break down and release their nutrients. Some, like blood, fish and bone, are a mixture of both.

For more or less foolproof feeding, a controlled-release fertilizer releases its nutrients over a period of up to six months. This makes just one feed at the start of the growing season all you need. Fertilizers are quite expensive, so check the recommended amount and stick to it. Don't be tempted to give the

> ❛ Soil needs feeding to make it fertile, so feed it every spring ❜

plants just a little bit more for good luck – not only would it be a waste of money, you could be doing more harm than good. When they are established, feed your plants every spring, just as they are starting to grow.

Changing the soil

In the small triangular bed next to the house in the Square garden, the soil was truly terrible, like the contents of a vacuum cleaner's dust bag! If you've got just one small area in the garden like this, you could dig it out and replace it with new soil. The best bet for covering a small area is to buy bags of John Innes No. 3, a soil-based compost which has been sterilized and so is free from weeds and pests.

Above: Double-digging a new border on clay lets you work in compost and grit to open up the soil.

Left: Organic matter can be forked in to feed the soil.

Far left: By digging gravel into the somewhat silty soil in the Square garden, we created ideal growing conditions for grey-leafed plants like catmint and Russian sage.

HOW AND WHAT TO PLANT

When you start to dig your planting holes, you may wonder why you have bothered to dig over the whole area first. The answer is simple. If you just dug a small hole in unprepared soil and slotted your plants in, they would be happy enough for a year or two, but then they would start to suffer as their roots moved out and either found impenetrable clay or thin, poor, starved soil. If you have heavy clay soil, they would suffer particularly badly because the holes you dug would simply act as sumps into which water would drain, leaving your newly planted trees and shrubs with their roots sitting in water and rotting.

The first job before you plant is to make sure that the plants are thoroughly watered while they're still in their pots. It's much easier to make sure the roots are really moist this way than it is by watering once they're in the ground.

If the water starts pouring out of the drainage holes almost at once, don't think that the job is done. The plant is probably so dry that the compost has shrunk away from the sides of the pot, and the water has just poured straight down the sides without wetting the compost and the roots at all.

The foolproof method is to plunge the pot into a bucket of water until the rim is just covered and hold it there until the bubbles have stopped rising. If the compost is very dry, the plant may float out of its pot. Just hold it in position until the compost is wet enough and heavy enough not to float.

With big pots that are too large to fit into a bucket, just water them slowly, giving them at least a watering can of water each, but lift them up before you start, to get a feeling of their weight. You can tell when the compost is thoroughly soaked because the pot will feel much heavier. Leave the plants to drain for a while – you want the roots moist but not waterlogged.

The next step is to lay out the plants on the soil, still in their pots, and see how they look. There are no hard and fast rules about arranging plants, but there are a few pointers to bear in mind.

Don't plant in straight lines. Stagger your shrubs, and, if you're using three of the same perennials to make a clump, plant them in a triangle.

If your selection includes evergreens, arrange them first because that will show you what the border will look like in winter, and then use them as a backdrop for your showier spring- and summer-flowering plants.

Think about the season in which the plants give their main show and group them accordingly. It may be tempting to spread them out so you get, say, bits of spring colour throughout the border, but you'll get a far greater impact by keeping them together. So if you've got 50 tulips to put in your garden, plant them in one large group rather than dotting them singly all over the place.

Size – both height and spread – are obviously important factors. You don't want to plant a small shrub behind a large one, but it's easy to make that mistake as they'll both be much the same size when you buy them. Look at the label to get an idea of how tall and how broad the plants will eventually become. Obviously you don't have to plant strictly according to height, and you get a more interesting effect if you don't. Something tall at the front of the border can look good as long as it's light, open and airy, like a grass such as golden oat grass (*Stipa gigantea*) through which you can see the smaller plants behind.

Leaving the right amount of space between plants is something new gardeners find very hard to do, and understandably. It's disappointing to spend time and money and finish up with vast stretches of bare soil between tiny, new shrubs. One answer is to plant more closely together and be prepared to cut back in a couple of years when they start growing into each other, or to dig some out and replant them somewhere else. Another is to leave the right amount of space between shrubs and fill the gaps with perennials which grow much more quickly but which can be moved easily once the shrubs are filling the space. Or you can fill the gaps with annuals that will only last for one season. Remember, though, that they will be competing with your shrubs for food and water, so make sure they all get a plentiful supply of both.

Right: Think carefully about how you combine plants so that their colours and shapes complement each other. The silvery lamb's ears work as well with the soft blue cornflowers as with the magenta of the geranium 'Ann Folkard'.

Having checked from several different angles that you are happy with the arrangement, remove the plants, marking their position with bamboo canes or labels. Starting with the permanent trees and shrubs, dig the first planting hole. Since you will have already prepared the border, this should be a piece of cake!

Make the hole at least twice the diameter of the pot and a little deeper. Add a few handfuls of organic matter and mix it with the soil at the bottom of the hole. Then sprinkle in half the fertilizer and scatter the rest on the pile of topsoil with which you're going to fill in the hole.

Put the plant, still in its pot, into the hole and check that the level is right. The soil should be level with the compost in the pot, especially if the plant has been grafted, as most roses and many other ornamental plants are. You can spot a graft easily enough – it's the nobbly lump low down on the main stem just above soil level. That must remain above the soil, because the plant is most vulnerable to rot and diseases at this point and also because if it's below the soil, the coarser root system could start producing unattractive suckers which will eventually swamp the cultivated plant.

Take it carefully out of its pot – as it's been well watered it should slip out easily. If not, just gently squeeze the sides of the pot and try again.

Sometimes at this point you'll discover that the plant has not been grown in its pot, but has just recently been 'potted up' because all the compost will fall away from the roots. In winter, when the plant is dormant, this is only irritating, but in spring or summer it's more serious because growing plants resent major disturbance to their roots. So hold the roots and compost together as best you can, get it into the hole quickly and keep an eye on it for the next few weeks, watering it copiously.

If the rootball of the plant stays intact, place it in the hole and move it around until its best side is facing the front. Yes, plants, like people, do have a best side. Then fill in the hole around the rootball with soil and fertilizer. Once the hole is half full,

⁶ Always water the plants well first ⁹

press gently with the ball of your foot to firm the soil and to make sure there are no air pockets around the roots. Finish filling in the hole, tread gently again and water thoroughly. Plant perennials and annuals in the same way.

Incidentally, don't panic if you find you've planted something in the wrong place. With newly planted trees and shrubs, you can either move them right away, within a week or two, or wait until late autumn, when they are dormant. You can also move shrubs that are well established, provided they're shallow-rooted varieties (see page 71).

Perennials are even more accommodating. As long as you give them a thorough soaking first, and make sure their new planting hole has had a thorough watering too, you can dig them up and move them even when they're in flower. They may look a bit floppy for a day or two, but they will quickly perk up again. We planted a bright red potentilla (*P.* 'Gibson's Scarlet') accidentally-on-purpose in among our pastels in the Oblong garden, moved it in midsummer in full flower and it's just fine.

Bulbs, which bring such a welcome splash of colour in the spring, are easy to plant. They look best in large groups and planted informally, not in straight lines like soldiers. Either mark out a drift on the soil and arrange the bulbs at the correct planting distance (look on the packet) within it. Or throw them onto the soil and plant them where they fall, though you may have to cheat a bit and rearrange them if they fall too close together. Where possible, plant bulbs in among other plants. This solves the problem of what to do with bulb foliage after flowering has finished and it's looking a mess. You can't cut them down for six weeks because they are manufacturing the food for next year's leaves and flowers. Planting them this way means the other plants' new leaves help hide their messy foliage and, what's more, you're far less likely to slice your bulbs in half when you're digging than you would be if they were planted in bare soil.

The rule for planting most spring-flowering bulbs is the same – make sure they have twice their own height of soil on top of them. A bulb that's 2.5cm (1in) tall needs 5cm (2in) of soil on top of it, so make your hole 7.5cm (3in) deep. With most bulbs, it's very obvious which way in they go – pointed end up – but with some tubers, like *Anemone blanda,* which look like gnarled bits of dried mushroom, you just have to push them into the soil and let them sort themselves out.

Small-species crocus like 'Blue Pearl' or 'Snowbunting', not the big Dutch hybrids, can look very attractive planted in grass. Use an old knife to make a hole in the lawn, wiggling it back and forth until it's wide enough, then push the bulb in to the correct depth and close up the hole again with your fingers. The bulbs flower in late winter and by the time you're ready to give the lawn its first cut of the spring, the leaves will be dying down and can be mown with no ill effects for next year's flowers.

Watering

Thorough watering is the key to successful planting. About half of all newly planted trees and shrubs die in the first year, mainly through lack of water. Most new gardeners are astonished at how much water plants need. Half a watering can or a few minutes with the hose will merely wet the surface and is nowhere near enough. Turn the hose on to a gentle trickle and leave it to run at the base of the tree or shrub for a couple of hours at the least.

Six good perennials for a shady border

Lady's mantle (*Alchemilla mollis*)

Japanese anemone (*Anemone x hybrida* 'Honorine Jobert') (or any)

Cranesbill (*Geranium macrorrhizum* 'Album') (or any) (S/E)

Hosta sieboldiana elegans

Lungwort (*Pulmonaria* 'Sissinghurst White')

Dead nettle (*Lamium maculatum* 'Beacon Silver') (or any) (E)

for a sunny border

Campanula persicifolia 'Telham Beauty'

Penstemon 'Apple Blossom' (or any)

Catmint (*Nepeta mussinii* or x *faassenii*) (E)

Euphorbia wulfenii (E)

Ox-eye chamomile (*Anthemis tinctoria* 'E. C. Buxton')

Lamb's ears (*Stachys olympica*) (E)

In the long term, the most efficient way to water – both in terms of the amount of water used and the effort expended – is with a soaker hose which gently seeps water along its length. Weave it between the plants and leave it in position, either covered with soil or with a mulch, so that the water goes exactly where it's most needed. All you do is turn on the tap for a couple of hours a day and the job is done.

Sprinklers are much less efficient because so much water evaporates in the air and, of course, it goes everywhere, not just where it's needed. And once the plants start to fill out, they act like an umbrella, keeping the water off the soil.

The best time to water is early morning or in the evening. If you water when the sun is out the evaporation is much greater and, besides, water drops left on leaves act like a magnifying glass so that the sun's rays scorch the foliage.

Staking trees

All new trees need staking, but the bamboo canes they're tied to when you buy them are just not strong enough to do the trick. It's now recognized that short stakes – about one third of the height of the trunk – are more efficient than the traditional, much longer ones. Allowing the top of the tree to sway about in the wind, it seems, thickens the base of the trunk and helps strengthen the root system more quickly.

You'll need a piece of timber

Left: Not only is the contrast between the deep, rich, blue flowers of the anchusa and the bright golden foliage of the elder (sambucus), a stunning one, but the contrast between the shapes of the leaves is also very attractive.

Above and left: Often, when the plant is very dry, water simply pours down the sides and out of the bottom of the pot, leaving the roots completely dry.

Right: The best way to ensure that the compost is thoroughly soaked is to put the plant in a bucket of water with the rim of the pot just submerged. You may find it trying to float out of its pot. Just hold it under the water until there are no more air bubbles.

measuring 5 x 5cm (2 x 2in) and pointed at one end. Measure the height of the trunk, divide by three (to give a third of its length) and then add 45cm (18in) to hammer into the ground.

Hammer the stake diagonally into the soil just behind the tree's rootball, keeping it close to the trunk. Attach the tree to the stake with a special adjustable tree tie that can be loosened as the trunk expands and which has a collar to go between the trunk and the stake to prevent chafing. Check the tie now and again to make sure it hasn't become too tight. Tree ties are very cheap but if you are on a very tight budget you could use a nylon stocking, tied in a figure of eight, to attach the tree to the stake. Whatever you do, though, don't use wire or nylon twine as this cuts into the bark as the tree grows and either allows diseases in or kills it outright.

What to choose

The key to growing plants successfully is not just in preparing the soil well and looking after them once they're in, but in choosing the right plants in the first place – ones that are best suited to the conditions in your garden. Obviously the sort of soil you have is one important factor, and is likely to apply to the whole garden, while the other key factor – the amount of sun and shade – will vary. Most gardens get a bit of both throughout the day, which gives you the chance to grow a wide range of different plants.

Six good shrubs for sun

Tree mallow (*Lavatera* 'Barnsley')

Ceanothus 'Blue Mound'

Mock orange blossom (*Philadelphus* 'Manteau d'Ermine')

Potentilla fruticosa 'Abbotswood' (or any)

Phormium cookianum 'Cream Delight' (E)

Butterfly bush (*Buddleja* 'Loch Inch') (or any small variety)

for shade

Euonymus fortunei 'Emerald Gaiety' (or any) (E)

False castor oil plant (*Fatsia japonica*) (E)

Golden cut-leafed elder (*Sambucus racemosa* 'Plumosa Aurea')

Flowering currant (*Ribes sanguineum* 'Pulborough Scarlet')

Firethorn (*Pyracantha* 'Orange Glow') (or any) (E)

Dogwood (*Cornus alba* 'Elegantissima')

But how do you know which plants thrive in which conditions? First, you could consult a good reference book which will tell you which conditions are best for particular plants. If you don't know what you want, consult a book that lists plants according to their preferred conditions and, having seen what will thrive, make your choice. Some garden centres make it very easy for you by dividing the plants up into separate sections for sun-lovers and shade-lovers, and all the good ones will label the plants with basic information about their requirements.

The only slight complication here can be deciding what 'part-shade' means. Is it an area that gets dappled sunlight all day, or is it one that gets full sun for half the day? I would say a spot that gets full sun all afternoon – in other words one that faces west – should be treated as a sunny spot, while dappled sunlight under trees and an east-facing spot that gets the morning sun, will suit plants that like 'part-shade', with the exception of shrubs such as camellias and Japanese maple (*Acer palmatum*) which can be damaged if the early morning sun thaws frozen flowers, buds or young leaves too quickly.

There are also some useful rules of thumb which you can apply to most plants though, inevitably, there are exceptions. Shade-loving plants, for example, tend to have large, thin leaves to make the most of any light available. Hostas, fatsias, ornamental rhubarb (*Rheum* 'Ace of Hearts'), elephant's ears (*bergenia*), are good examples. Ferns come into this category, too, because their fronds, although finely divided, cover a large surface area. The leaves of shade-lovers, evergreens in particular, also tend to be shiny, like laurel (*Prunus laurocerasus*), camellias and ivies (*hedera*), again to make maximum use of available light by reflecting it around. The shiny coating often indicates plants that can cope with dry shade, since it also helps keep in moisture.

Sun-lovers on the other hand tend to have very narrow leaves, such as lavender (*lavendula*) and rosemary (*rosmarinus*) or skeletal ones like artemisias, and most of them are covered with a protective coating of very fine hairs that gives them a grey or silver colouring. In fact, apart from the silvery dead nettles (*lamium*) and lungworts (*pulmonaria*), which are happy in shade, anything with silver leaves needs full sun. Plants with fleshy leaves like the ice-plant (*Sedum spectabile*) and succulents like cacti must also have full sun.

Choose a flowering plant with the most buds, rather than the most flowers

Golden foliage almost always needs part-shade as full sun will scorch the leaves and full shade will not bring out the golden colour, though the plant may well survive in a duller lime-green version.

On the whole, the hotter the flower colour the more sun it needs, so vibrant magentas, pinks, scarlets and yellows need a sunny spot, while shade-lovers tend to have small flowers in pastel shades such as pinks, blues, mauves and whites.

Most bedding plants need plenty of sun, with the notable exceptions of busy lizzies (*impatiens*), lobelias, begonias and fuchsias.

Maximum impact

In a large garden, you can indulge yourself in plants that give a wonderful show for a couple of weeks, but then do nothing for the rest of the year. In a small garden, though, you really need to choose plants that will earn their keep by providing maximum impact for as long as possible – either by flowering for months on end or by having attractive foliage, too, or good autumn colour or attractive bark in winter. If you want a climbing rose, for instance, choose a repeat-flowering variety rather than one that only flowers for a couple of weeks. If you want to grow a dogwood (*Cornus alba*) for the bright red stems it displays in winter, choose one with very attractive foliage in summer like the pale green and cream variegated *C. a.* 'Elegantissima' or the golden variegated 'Spaethii'. Do remember that on the whole, foliage gives you a much longer season of interest than flowers, so look for at least some plants with interesting foliage to provide a foil for the flowering plants. I have to say, though, that most new gardeners just want masses of colourful flowers in their first garden and a love of subtle foliage is something that seems to develop later in life!

You might think that in a small garden you ought to stick to small plants, but don't be afraid of using some very large plants. They can give you instant and dramatic impact while your newly planted permanent trees and shrubs are still very small and, being purely practical, they also fill a lot of space very cheaply. If you choose perennials that die down each autumn and reappear the following spring, or even annuals that only live for one summer rather than shrubs or trees, you won't be creating problems for yourself long term because they will never outgrow their allotted space.

We planted a cardoon (*Cynara cardunculus*) in the City garden, which grew in just a few months to tree-like proportions – over 2m (6ft 7in) in height with dramatic jagged silvery leaves about 1m (40in) long and stunning blue thistle flowers. The cardoon is a perennial, and by the end of the summer, although its main stem had died back, it was already producing bright, silvery new leaves for next year. It had done its job, though, and while Catherine felt considerably warmer towards it once it produced its flowers, she didn't think it had a

Left: All young trees need staking while they get established. Stout stakes one-third the height of the trunk have been shown to be more effective than traditional, taller ones because they allow the tree to move in the wind, which helps thicken up the trunk and establish a strong root system.

Below: Some of the main permanent ingredients of this border set out ready to plant: a climber – Solanum crispum *'Glasnevin'; a single-stemmed tree – the winter-flowering cherry (*Prunus subhirtella *'Autumnalis'); multi-stemmed shrubs – Burkwood's viburnum (V. x burkwoodii) with white balls of flower, and a shrubby mallow (*Lavatera *'Barnsley'); and perennials like hardy geraniums (G. 'Ann Folkard') which die back or disappear in winter but come back again in spring.*

*Right: The same border three months later, with the addition of some permanent silvery lamb's ears (*Stachys olympica*), and a few packets of hardy annual seeds.*

long-term role in the garden, so out it came. Other good big, dramatic perennials include ornamental rhubarb (*Rheum* 'Ace of Hearts'), rodgersias (if your soil is moist), crambe (*C. cordifolia*), which has huge cabbage-like leaves and a tall spike carrying clouds of tiny white flowers, and the plume poppy (*Macleaya cordata*), which will reach up to 2.5m (8ft) in a season. Tall, ornamental grasses like miscanthus are also a good bet because they give you instant height, but unlike bamboo, which looks vaguely similar, they die back in winter, reappear the following spring and aren't invasive.

In the Oblong garden, we sowed a large patch of pale creamy yellow sunflowers (*helianthus*), called 'Italian White', which grew to 2m (6ft 7in) plus. Courgettes are excellent for this purpose, too – a packet of seeds costs very little, you can germinate them easily on a windowsill and, finally, you get an edible bonus.

Colour

The choice of colour in the garden, as in your home and in your wardrobe, is intensely personal and all that matters, ultimately, is that you like it. But if you think about any lovely garden you know, you'll find that colour is a crucial element in why it looks so good and you'll find, too, that it has been used with a great deal of thought.

When it comes to choosing colours, people often forget about green, and yet it is the main colour in any garden. I say 'green', but of course that covers forty shades from deep, dark green through emerald green, apple green, blue green, sage green, moss green to lime green. It's also a very cool, restful colour and gardens that are predominantly green are relaxing to be in. One of the most effective planting schemes for a tiny, shady city yard, for instance, is primarily glossy evergreen foliage such as ivies (*hedera*), fatsia, Mexican orange blossom (*Choisya ternata*), and white flowers like busy lizzies (*impatiens*), Japanese anemones (*Anemone japonica*) and again the Mexican orange blossom.

There is a school of thought that says no colours in nature can possibly clash, so you can grow any plant with any other and still get a harmonious effect. That's true of wild plants maybe, but it certainly isn't true of the many modern hybrids bred by plant scientists. Screaming magenta and vibrant orange is just one of the more horrendous combinations that spring to mind.

If you want to enjoy being in your garden, use colour judiciously, as you would in your home. You're unlikely to want canary yellow walls, deep purple upholstery, emerald green carpet, scarlet curtains and sky blue cushions in your living room, are you? So why have the same migraine-inducing jumble in your garden? Using blocks of single colours will have far more impact than using lots of different ones and dotting them about.

Think about colour themes for different parts of the garden. The pale colours – the ever-popular pale blues, pinks, mauves, whites and silvers – are relaxing, so use them where you like to sit. They are also the ones that look best in evening light, so plant them where you will spend most time in the garden late in the day. Hot colours look best in bright sunlight, so place them where they can be enjoyed in the middle of the day. They're also stimulating, so use them where there's most likely to be activity – round a barbecue for instance.

As for colour combinations, it may help to look at a colour wheel which shows the six pure colours as segments – yellow, green, blue, purple, red and orange. Colours next to each other – orange and yellow, yellow and green – harmonize, while colours opposite each other – blue and orange, yellow and purple – contrast. The colours in the 'hot' half of the wheel – red, orange and yellow – will also work well together, as will those in the cool half – green, blue and purple. Strength of colour is also a factor to consider. While you still have to use strong colours with care, most pastel shades – blues, pinks, whites, mauves and pale yellows – work very well together.

You can use both bright colours and pastels if you want to, but not all mixed up together. Separate them either with foliage – green, silver, gold or even purple – or white flowers, or with a shade that works with both groups. A soft buttery yellow, for instance, would look equally good with pastels as with richer golds. In the sunny border of our Oblong garden, we started with hot yellows and reds nearest the house, and moved through lemon yellow daisies (*Anthemis tinctoria* 'E. C. Buxton') into blues, pinks and whites, ending with the mass of sunflowers (*helianthus*) at the end of the garden.

Think carefully about the tone of your colours, since each one covers a wide spectrum. Pink, for instance, ranges from nearly blue-mauve to almost orange-salmon, which look awful together. Blue-reds look very good with purple; orange-reds don't.

These few principles are really just to help you get started but, of course, like all rules, they are there to be broken. I planted a late-flowering wine-red clematis on a fence only to find some of the bright orange crocosmia I thought I'd dug out flowering just in front of it. On paper it shouldn't have worked. In the garden, it looked sensational. So don't be afraid to experiment. If you buy a new plant in flower, put it with established plants, still in its pot, and see if you like the effect. If you do, that's all that matters.

What to buy

Before you set off for the garden centre, make a list of suitable plants with several alternative choices in each category. You won't stick to it entirely, but at least that way you won't be buying everything on impulse. Without the discipline of a list, the danger is that you buy only the plants that are in flower and looking wonderful just then, so that you wind up with a garden that looks good at that time of year, and really boring for the other 50 weeks.

To make sure that you buy the very best plants, go to a garden centre with a good reputation, which looks well cared for and which has a large selection of plants on offer. If the place looks run down and scruffy, with only a few tatty plants to choose from, go somewhere else.

Pick up the plants and look at them carefully. Have they been well watered or are they dry as dust? Do they look healthy? Is there any sign of disease or pests on the leaves? Is there moss or lichen growing on the compost or are there lots of roots coming out of the bottom of the pot? Both are signs that the plant has been in its pot rather a long time and so could be starved of nutrients, which means it will take some time to recover.

If you are buying roses in leaf in the spring, make sure that they are container-grown, and not just containerized. If they are container-grown, you should be able to lift up the whole works – rose, compost, container – by the top growth, because the plant has a well established root system which means it will transplant into your garden very happily. If the rose starts to come out of the compost as soon as you try to lift it, it is a bare-rooted rose which has only been potted up very recently. As you try to plant it, the compost will fall away, disturbing the immature root system and making it more difficult for the plant to get established. It's absolutely fine to plant bare-rooted roses in winter BEFORE they start into growth, but not once they've started growing. Container-grown roses are also more expensive, so it's a bit of a rip-off, too.

Given that all the specimens of a particular shrub on offer are healthy, how do you know which one to choose? Most new gardeners, understandably, would go for the tallest as best value for money but that's unlikely to be the best buy. What you want is the bushiest plant on offer, the one with the most stems, and the one with an attractive, well-balanced shape. If it's a flowering plant, look to the future rather than the present, and choose the one with the most buds, not the one with the most flowers.

Many garden centres have a bargain section and, like all 'bargains', you should approach them with care. If it's late summer, for instance, annuals or half-hardy perennials like geraniums and osteospermums which won't survive the winter outside are not much of a bargain even if they are still looking very good because they only have another few weeks to live. On the other hand, perennials which look pretty tatty after a summer in a pot can be real bargains because they will come back year after year. If you're not sure which category a particular plant falls into, ask a member of staff. If they seem unsure – and that can happen – get them to look it up, or look it up yourself in a good reference book.

OUT TO GRASS

Above: Having damaged the lawn in our Square garden while reshaping it, we patched it with pieces of surplus lawn. It's not as easy as laying proper turf, but it does blend with the existing grass more quickly.

Left: Hard landscaping need not look hard if you leave gaps in which to plant low-growing alpines and herbs.

Inset, top: Essential for revitalising a badly compacted lawn, aerating with the hollow-tined fork improves drainage and allows air to reach the roots.

Inset, bottom: The next stage is to work turf dressing, a mixture of sharp sand, fine soil and compost into the holes you've made to keep the soil free-draining, and an old doormat, weighted with bricks, is an excellent way of making sure that happens.

There is no doubt that a lawn is the best surface in most back gardens. You can sit on it, sunbathe on it or practise your putting on it. Children and dogs can play on it, too. It's certainly the cheapest form of surface there is, though it is not, contrary to popular belief, a low-maintenance option. Lawns can become a way of life to some men (that's not sexist, it's true – I have never encountered a female lawn fanatic in my life) who devote all their spare time and money to producing something that makes the Centre Court at Wimbledon look like rough meadow.

I'm assuming that you want a lawn that you can use, on which people are actually allowed to walk (yes, I have met lawn fanatics who don't even allow their own wives to set foot on the lawn), sit in a deckchair or even kick a football – one that looks good enough to be an asset to the garden and not a liability. Many of the problems with lawns spring from the fact that most people simply think of lawn as 'lawn', not as thousands of grass plants that need food, water and air to thrive just like any other plant. Once you know that, you shouldn't find it difficult to sort out many of the common problems and keep the lawn in good enough heart.

The first thing to do is assess what you have already got and identify the problems. You will almost certainly have weeds – plantains, dandelions, daisies, and so on – some moss and probably some coarse grass, as well as some proper, finer lawn grasses. I would be lying if I said that any lawn could be salvaged, because some are so far gone that the only solution is to start again. But it is true to say that most lawns can be brought back to an acceptable condition with a bit of remedial work, regular cutting and a willingness to accept a few weeds and a bit of moss, as long as the lawn looks green from a distance! And for new gardeners it's certainly worth trying that approach first.

The lawn in our Oblong garden had its fair share of problems. There were masses of weeds, the grass was very thin in parts and there were a number of completely bald patches. Some were explicable – those by the bottom of the steps down from the patio, for instance, were clearly the result of wear and tear, but others further down the garden were more baffling. At first, we wondered whether Martin and Susan's two large dogs were responsible, but they are dogs and it's bitches' urine that scorches grass.

Certainly, one cause of the generally poor state of the grass here and in many gardens was thatch. This is the layer of dead vegetation – grass clippings, leaves and moss – which builds up on the soil at the base of the grass, depriving it of light, air and water. You need to rake it all out with a spring-tined rake (see page 17), and spring is the best time to do it. If you do it properly, it leaves the lawn looking pretty battered, but it's for its own good! Another common cause of poor, sparse lawns, and certainly the case here, is compaction. Most lawns get trodden on year after year so the soil becomes compacted, making it impossible for air to get to the roots or for water to drain away – so that, in effect, the roots are drowning.

To prevent this, you need to aerate the lawn by making lots of small holes about 12–15cm (5–6in) deep, which improves the drainage and allows air to reach the roots. You can do it with a garden fork, wiggled back and forth to enlarge the holes. If you have a large area to cover or a really serious compaction problem, you can hire a hollow-tined fork, which is rather like a multi-pronged pogo stick and removes cores of soil, depositing them on the surface. Make rows about 12cm (5in) apart.

Afterwards, brush away any soil on the surface and apply a top dressing – a mixture of good, sieved garden soil, sharp sand (but not ordinary builders' sand which will just make the problem worse) and compost – which you can mix up yourself or buy ready mixed from the garden centre. If the lawn is pretty sparse, then mix some grass seed into the top dressing – about 10 handfuls to a 25-litre sack is about right. Dump a good spadeful of mixture for every square metre or so and level it roughly with the back of a rake. You really need to work it down into the holes, so either brush it with a besom, or use an old door mat, weighted down with bricks

> *Just like any other plant, grass needs air, light, food and water*

and attached to some rope, and drag it over the lawn. If it doesn't rain during the following few days, put the lawn sprinkler on for a few hours to make sure the top dressing is well down into the holes and to start the grass seed germinating.

Weeds

Almost every lawn has weeds and, given how much work is involved in getting rid of every single one, it's a question really of deciding what proportion you can tolerate. The most effective form of general weed control is mowing. Broad-leafed weeds can't cope with having their leaves sliced off every week and so soon give up the ghost. Grass, on the other hand, responds very well to regular cutting, growing more and more strongly and freezing out the competition. If your lawn is a mass of weeds, though, it's also worth treating it with a weed-and-feed mixture – weedkiller to deal with the weeds and fertilizer to help the grass grow strongly and fill in the resulting gaps.

If you only have a few weeds, however, treat them individually. Some shallow-rooted ones like plantains can be dug out with an old kitchen knife but others, like dandelions, which are very deep rooted, need a different treatment. You could use a special tool which twists them out of the ground very effectively, or try a spot weedkiller which you simply dab into the centre of the rosette of leaves, although it may take more than one application to kill it. If you don't want to use chemicals, try ordinary kitchen salt sprinkled on the centre of the rosette, though use it carefully since it will kill the surrounding grass, too, if you spill it.

Moss

Moss grows on poorly drained, shady lawns where the grass isn't strong enough to defend itself. The only way to get rid of it is to use a moss killer which turns it black, after which you rake it out. Don't ever rake out living moss, though, since you simply spread it to the parts it hasn't yet reached by itself. After this treatment, you must improve the state of your lawn or the moss will be back! At least moss is green and springy to walk on and, provided there's not too much of it, you could do worse than just live with it.

Feeding and watering

Grass needs feeding just like any other plant. You can use a granular feed, which you apply dry. If there's no rain after two days, you must water it in or it will scorch the grass. Alternatively, you can use a liquid feed, preferably with a special hose-end feeder, which automatically dilutes the fertilizer to the right strength as you water. The best time to feed is in the spring as the grass begins to grow strongly. If you feed it again in midsummer, you won't need to feed again in the autumn.

Watering is also vital for a healthy lawn and for this you must have a sprinkler. The nozzle on the hose or a watering can simply can't give it the amount it needs. And a little water is worse than none because it brings thirsty roots up to the surface where they are even more vulnerable to drying out. If you can't water because there's a hose pipe ban, then don't cut the grass and don't worry that it turns brown. Grass is remarkably resilient and will perk up quite quickly once it gets some water again.

Mowing

From spring to autumn, when the grass is growing, a lawn needs mowing once a week – ideally twice a week in the middle of summer when it's growing most vigorously. It needs less mowing in dry weather or if it's in shade. Never cut it too short or you may scalp it, leaving bare patches of soil which

are the perfect breeding ground for weeds and moss. If you can't cut it for a few weeks, because it's too wet or you're away, make sure the first cut only takes a little off the top. If you take off too much in one go, it's a real shock to its system. If you find lots of worm casts on your lawn, brush them off before you mow, otherwise the mower flattens them into little seedbeds of fine soil for weeds. Don't, whatever you do, kill the worms – they are valuable friends.

If you use a rotary or a cylinder mower, try to mow in a different direction each time, since these mowers tend to flatten the grass in the direction you're mowing.

Repairs

In our Square garden, the grass was in slightly better condition. However, once we had reshaped it and put in a brick mowing edge (you can run the mower straight over it so you don't have to spend time trimming the edges), there was a small area in need of patching. Since we had removed a lot of lawn in the reshaping, there was plenty of turf available for the purpose and, of course, since it was the same grass, it would blend in with the existing lawn right away.

> *Regular mowing kills off most broad-leafed weeds*

To make life simpler, the grass around the area to be patched should be cut away to make a square or oblong shape with good clean edges. Lay pieces of turf over the gap and trim them carefully with a garden knife (or old bread knife) to fit.

Before you actually lay the turf, prepare the soil well by digging it over, removing any stones and then consolidating it to give a good, firm, flat base. The best way to do this in such a small area is by treading it or jumping up and down on it. You will feel very silly so ideally do it when you know the neighbours aren't in! If the soil is very dry, water the area first using the very fine spray or the watering can with the rose on.

Left and below: The dullest suburban strip can be transformed for free by reshaping the lawn. Cutting it into generous, sweeping curves draws your eye across the garden, emphasizing the width rather than the length. Either draw a plan to scale and, using the boundaries as fixed points, mark out the shape with a tape-measure and pegs, or do it by eye using a hose pipe to make the curves. The generous curves of the lawn also create deeper borders, allowing you to plant in bigger groups than straight and narrow ones would.

Above: As long as you leave room for lots of plants, a combination of paving and gravel can be a very attractive alternative when a lawn just isn't practical.

Right: Consolidating soil with cement to make a firm base for gravel is one of the cheapest and easiest forms of hard landscaping there is.

Unlike commercially grown turf, recycled bits of old lawn aren't of a uniform thickness, so you may need to add a bit more soil under any obvious dips. Press the patches hard up against each other because there is bound to be some shrinkage. If gaps do appear later, fill them with soil and the grass should colonize them in time.

Once the patches are laid, bang them down hard with the back of a rake to force the roots into close contact with the soil, and encourage them to take hold as quickly as possible. After the patching is complete, put the sprinkler on the lawn for a couple of hours, and keep it well watered until the patches have taken. In a few weeks, you really won't be able to see the join.

The mysterious bald patches in the Oblong garden continued to be a problem. In one area, we tried a new product which consists of grass seed contained in a mat of wood fibre which can be used either to lay whole new lawns or for patching. We first prepared the soil by breaking up the top layer and then levelling it, then cut a piece of mat to fit the bare patch and kept it well watered. By the end of the summer it was growing well and you had to look quite hard to see the join! In the autumn, we gave the lawn some special autumn lawn food which doesn't make the grass grow – the last thing you want in winter – but strengthens the roots so it will survive the winter in good shape.

New lawns

We were able to revitalize the existing grass in the Square and Oblong gardens, but if yours is beyond redemption, then start again, either with seed or turf. Seed is much cheaper but takes longer to get established than turf. Spring or autumn are the ideal times, because the soil is warm, and it's more likely to rain. The preparation for both turf and seed is the same.

Never mow too short – scalping the lawn lets in weeds and moss

First, get rid of the existing grass with a glyphosate weedkiller, which kills grass and weeds completely but is inactive in the soil. Once it's dead, which can take a few weeks, dig it over, finely chopping up the dead vegetation with the spade and working it into the soil as organic matter. Level it roughly with a rake or the back of a fork.

Next, compact it to remove any air pockets by treading all over with your weight on your heels. You do feel extremely silly as you shuffle along, but it's the only way to do it properly.

Then feed it – with blood, fish and bone or growmore – and rake it again carefully. You may wonder why you're loosening up the soil again after all that compacting but you are just opening up the top layer of soil ready for the seed or the roots of the turf. It's also the last chance to get rid of those awkward little dips that the lawnmower will always miss later – crouch down every few metres as you rake and look along the ground to spot any areas that aren't level.

Turf

Order the best turf you can afford from a reputable supplier and have it delivered the day before you plan to lay it so it won't dry out. You'll need a rake and a scaffold plank (hire or borrow one) as you mustn't stand on newly laid turf or prepared soil.

Start with the longest straight side and lay the first row of turf. Bang it down with the back of the rake to ensure the roots are in close contact with the soil. Standing on the scaffold plank placed over the first row, lay the second row, making sure you butt it right up against the first, since turf is inclined to shrink. You'll probably have some trimming and patching to do at the ends of rows or on curves. Just lay the patching turf over the one already laid, locate the edge and trim it with an old knife. Make sure it never dries out – water it every day if there is no rain. It'll take between a few days and a few weeks for the turf to root, but you can tell when it has because the grass starts looking perkier and a much fresher green colour.

Seed

Choose the right seed – bowling green or heavy duty, sun or shade or half and half. Sow when the soil is drying out but still moist – a few hours after a shower or a session with the sprinkler. Sow it at the rate of 45g (2oz) to the square metre. Weigh out the seed, pour into a jam jar and mark the level with a pen. Then refill the jar with seed to that line.

You don't need to divide the whole lawn into squares with string and bamboo canes – just mark out one square metre in the soil with a stick and scatter the grass seed over it as evenly as possible to see what the right density looks like. When you're sowing, stand with your feet about a metre apart and stretch out your hand as far as you can. The area in front of you is roughly a square metre.

Once you've sown the seed, rake it in lightly with a spring-tined rake. Aim to cover about half the seed with soil. Don't water it – that could form a hard crust which would prevent germination or make hollows and wash the seed into them. Discourage birds with strips of kitchen foil tied to bamboo canes which rattle and flash in the light.

Don't cut new grass until it is at least 5cm (2in) tall then cut it with the mower blades at their highest setting and gradually reduce the height over the next few mowings.

Alternatives to lawns

If your garden is a small city yard, you probably won't have a lawn and it certainly isn't worth the effort and expense of digging up concrete to create one. Even if there is a lawn, it may not be practical to keep it, especially in a very small garden where it gets too much wear and tear, or when there's too much shade or nowhere to keep a mower.

That was the case with our City garden and, with a toddler and dog wanting to use it all year round,

hard landscaping was a much more practical proposition. A lot of new gardeners resist the idea because they think that hard landscaping must look bleak but, provided you have lots of plants in beds and containers, you can have a stunningly pretty garden you can use all year round and which is also very easy to maintain.

There is a wide choice of hard landscaping materials available now – setts, tiles, decking, as well as bricks and slabs – to suit all tastes, styles and bank balances, and many of them designed for DIY. You'll get a more aesthetically pleasing garden if you choose materials that blend with or complement your house – bricks the same colour as the house bricks or neutral slabs. Lots of different materials in a small space look too busy.

Gravel is cheap and versatile. If you have a concrete yard and don't want the expense of digging it up, just spreading a thin layer of gravel on top will greatly improve the way it looks. You can lay gravel on soil, too, but it's not very functional in winter when it gets muddy. Instead, provide a weatherproof base by working dry cement into the soil – about one 25kg bag to 5 square metres – and then compact it, ideally with a vibrating plate (available from hire shops) or with a tamping board. The moisture in the soil rises up to set the cement and form a good, solid base for a thin layer of gravel.

In the City garden, we used a mixture of gravel and reproduction York stone slabs in different sizes. Using gravel in gaps between the slabs and at the edges of the beds means you won't need to cut any slabs, making the job much simpler. Another advantage of loose gravel is that you can grow plants through it, which softens the hard landscaping. We planted chamomile (*Anthemis nobilis*) and thyme (*thymus*) in the larger gaps where they are ideal as they don't mind being trodden on occasionally. Gravel is also the perfect place to grow alpines without building a rockery. So we planted a saxifrage (*saxifraga*) in an out-of-the-way space, since it doesn't like being trodden on. You can also sow seed directly into gravel if there's soil beneath. Californian poppies (*Eschscholzia californica*) do well in gravel and, since they are rampant self-seeders, you need sow them only once.

THE SNIP

Pruning keeps plants in good health and produces strong, vigorous new growth. This growth results in bigger or more plentiful flowers or, in the case of shrubs or trees grown for their foliage, the biggest and most brightly coloured leaves. And yet it is the one job in the garden that seems to throw beginners – and even some more experienced gardeners – into complete panic. They are all terrified that they are somehow going to do it wrong and kill their prize plants. And, given that there are whole volumes published on the subject, full of immensely complicated drawings, who can blame them for feeling nervous?

Once you have grasped a few basic guidelines, (why you prune and when is the best time to do it),

it really isn't so difficult. In fact, with very few exceptions, doing something in the way of pruning, even if it's not absolutely right, is generally better for the plant than doing nothing at all.

The worst case

The worst thing that could happen is that in very, very exceptional circumstances you could kill a plant by pruning it badly or at the wrong time, although I can't actually think of a single example from my own experience. Hard pruning may finish off a very old, badly neglected plant, but then you wouldn't want to keep it in that state anyway.

The next most dreadful thing that can happen, particularly if you prune at the wrong time, is that you will lose one season's flowers. If you take a long-term view, though, this is not necessarily a bad thing because you will be producing a healthier, more vigorous plant so the following year it will undoubtedly flower better than ever before!

Left: The overgrown laurel in the corner of our Square garden was too big for the space, but it gave privacy and an attractive evergreen background, so taking it out wasn't an option.

Below: We pruned it back very hard in mid-spring – the best time for evergreens, since they're just starting into growth – and four months later it had grown back so vigorously that it was ready for another trim.

This chapter covers the pruning of the most common garden shrubs – hybrid tea and floribunda roses, climbers, clematis, early and late summer-flowering shrubs like mock orange (*philadelphus*), lilac (*syringa*) and the butterfly bush (*buddleja*), as well as evergreens. It does not cover ornamental trees (mature ones are best left to professional tree surgeons) or fruit trees because, apart from removing dead and diseased wood, their pruning is a little more complicated – something, perhaps, not to tackle until you are more experienced.

> ❛ *Pruning produces better flowers and foliage and keeps plants small and vigorous* ❜

Step-by-step pruning

The first step with all trees and shrubs is the removal of dead wood. It's very easy to spot dead wood on evergreens at any time of year – it either has no leaves or dead ones – or on deciduous trees and shrubs (those that shed their leaves in autumn) in the summer when they are in leaf. In the winter, however, it is not as immediately obvious since, at first glance, the whole plant looks dead. Even then, though, dead wood is often a darker colour than the rest, as well as being very brittle, snapping easily if you try to bend it. If you are really not sure whether it's alive or dead, scrape away a little of the bark with your thumb nail. If it is bright green underneath, the wood is alive. If not, it's dead and you should cut it back to the point where it joins any live wood.

The next step is to remove any wood that is diseased. It will be clear that something is wrong because this wood looks different from all the rest. You should not only cut it right out, you should also burn it to prevent the spread of disease.

Next, take out any weak or spindly growths – they aren't productive and will sap the plant's energy. You should also cut out any branches that cross or rub against each other because the bark will be damaged, allowing diseases in.

Then prune out some of the old wood – usually easy to spot because it is 'woodier', darker and stiffer than the new growth – because this will not produce such large blooms or leaves as the new wood.

How much old wood you remove depends on the type of shrub. With some very common shrubs, such as lavender (*lavendula*), rosemary (*rosmarinus*) and broom (*cytisus/genista*), pruning cannot really rejuvenate old, neglected specimens. They won't produce strong, healthy new growth from wood that is two years old or more or, if they do, it will take several years for them to do so, and they will look a dreadful mess in the meantime. So, if you have an ancient lavender with lots of bare, gnarled old stems and just a bit of growth on the top, it is really better to dig it out and start all over again with a new plant. Once it's in, clip it over every spring, removing any dead flower spikes and the top of last season's growth. That will ensure that the plant doesn't become leggy and that the growth is always coming from new wood.

Feeding

Pruning is a real shock to any plant's system and it is just this shock that encourages it to start producing new growth. To make sure the new growth is really vigorous and healthy, though, and the plant doesn't exhaust itself in the growing process, you must feed it immediately after pruning, either with an organic fertilizer like pelleted chicken manure or an inorganic one like rose fertilizer, which is just as good for other shrubs as it is for roses.

The root system of most shrubs will extend about as widely below the ground as the canopy of its branches spread above before you started pruning, so spread the fertilizer over all the surrounding soil and work it in to the top layer with a fork. Work gently to avoid damaging any shallow roots.

Watering

Plants also need to be well watered after pruning. As well as providing moisture, watering also dissolves the fertilizer, making the nutrients available to the plant. Turn the hose on to a gentle trickle and leave it on next to the plant for at least an hour. You could make a small wall of soil around the area to keep the water where it will do most good – right above the root system.

Rose bushes

A tale to give you confidence. At the Royal National Rose Society's gardens in St. Albans, they have been conducting an experiment over the last five years with three identical beds of roses. Those in the first bed have been pruned correctly with secateurs, the second bed's have been pruned badly with secateurs and those in the third bed have been hacked with an electric hedge trimmer. And which roses have flowered best consistently over the five years? The ones pruned with a hedge trimmer! I'm not suggesting that you should prune your roses this way – though they do produce more flowers, the hacked bushes themselves look a real mess – but the lesson to be learned is that you really don't have to worry about getting it wrong because most roses, and indeed shrubs, particularly well established ones, are incredibly resilient and forgiving – and at the end of the day very hard to kill.

The rose is by far the most popular flower and almost every new gardener inherits at least one old rose bush, most likely a hybrid tea or floribunda, still producing a few flowers, but either untouched for years or badly chopped about. The rose in our City garden was typical. It was about 3m (10ft) high and produced some small pink and cream flowers but it was a real mess due basically to neglect.

The best time to prune roses is early spring before they start into growth, though you can prune later in the spring after the rose has already started to produce leaves – as we did. The only effect is that it will start flowering later.

The place to start tackling a neglected rose is not at the top, but at the bottom, where the basic structure of the bush is most obvious. This approach saves time. There is no point in pruning off lots of twiggy shoots or dead bits from the top if the whole stem will be coming out.

First of all, take out the dead and diseased wood. Then look at the old wood. It's easy to tell old wood on roses because it is brown, thick and doesn't have many thorns. Cut out about half of the oldest stems right back to the base of the plant. Then the following spring you can cut out the other half, so that you have renovated the rose completely. It takes courage, but you will be rewarded very quickly, in just a few weeks, with strong, healthy new growth shooting up from the base. Cut the remainder back to a point just above a younger shoot.

Next, look at the newer, greener wood on the rose. The object of pruning here is as much to create a good shape as it is to promote better flowering. The shape you want is a cup with an open centre and all the growth shooting outwards. Look for an outward-facing bud, which looks like a little dot just above a leaf scar – a thin line – on the outside of the stem. If you really aren't sure what a leaf bud looks like, find a leaf and pull it off to see what a fresh one is like. Then look down the stem for an older, more weathered version. Aim to prune about a third of the length of each shoot but, if the first outward-facing bud is lower down, prune just above it anyway.

As all the manuals will tell you, the ideal pruning cut is on a downward slant, at an angle of about 45° starting about 1cm (⅓in) above the bud. It slopes away from the bud so that any water runs off it, and not down into the bud which would encourage it to rot. A cut closer to the bud could damage it, while one much further away would leave too much of a stump which could die back into the new

> *You will not kill anything merely by pruning badly*

Right: Many new gardeners will have an old neglected rose bush to tackle. The trick is to start at the bottom, not the top, and take out all dead or diseased wood, and any branches that cross or rub. Then take out about half of the old wood. A small pruning saw will do the job more easily than secateurs.

Centre left: Prune young green wood back by a third to an outward facing bud so the new growth will shoot outwards.

Left: Prune out the dead and diseased wood first.

Above: Three metres (10ft) of old rose reduced to a small brown stump. It needs a good feed and copious watering to help it recover from major surgery.

Right: All Catherine needs is faith.

wood. If panic starts to set in, though, remember the Great St. Albans hedge-trimmer massacre and just go ahead and do it!

Once you have pruned your first rose, you may well be convinced that you have killed it. Have faith! Less than three months after pruning, Catherine's rose was full of new, healthy bronze-green growth, and covered in plentiful and bigger, brighter flowers than she had ever seen before.

With a rose that is not as overgrown or neglected, treatment doesn't need to be as radical. However, all roses need to have dead, diseased, spindly and some old wood removing each year and their newer growth pruning back by a third.

When your roses are back in shape, the rule of thumb is that weak growth should be pruned harder than strong growth. Floribundas (which carry their flowers in clusters) are more vigorous than hybrid teas (which carry theirs singly) and so should be pruned more lightly – back to four or five buds. The same is true within an individual rose bush. Prune strong growth back to four or five buds, and weaker growth to two or three.

Most plants will do better if pruned incorrectly than if they are not pruned at all

Neglected shrub roses and 'old-fashioned' roses, which tend to be bigger and bushier than modern hybrids, need slightly different treatment. They flower best on side shoots that develop from the previous year's growth. So, once you have cut out any dead, diseased or damaged wood, cut back any side shoots that have borne flowers to two buds from the point where they join the main stem, and just 'tip' the rest – remove the top few centimetres of growth – to encourage side shoots to form.

Climbing and rambling roses

The difference between climbers and ramblers is, very simply, that climbers have stiffer growth, are less vigorous and flower right through the summer. Ramblers are much more vigorous – they're the ones you see racing up tall trees – with much more flexible stems, but they usually only flower once in early to midsummer.

If your climbers are growing on walls or fences, create a basic framework for them where the branches are evenly spaced out in a rough fan shape from which the side shoots – the ones that will eventually produce flowers – can grow (see pages 21–25 for methods of supporting roses). If the climber already has a pretty good framework, take out one or two of the oldest shoots, right back to the base in early spring, then either trim back the newer side shoots to two or three buds or tie them horizontally to their wire supports. This will encourage the plant to produce vertical shoots, giving better coverage of the wall or fence and enabling it to produce more flowers.

If the climber is a bit of a mess, kit yourself out with stout gauntlets (gloves that stop at the wrist are not enough) and untie it from its support, gently untangling the main growths. It may be flexible enough to lay it on the ground and sort it out there, but most climbers are too stiff for that. Cut out one or two of the oldest, thickest stems and any that grow away from the fence, then tie the rest back in, as widely spaced as possible. Finally, tie in the newer, more flexible growths.

Ramblers are pruned quite differently. Although they will do very well for some years without pruning, if they get too dense and tangled their flowering declines, so it pays to take out some of the old wood. Prune as soon as they've finished flowering, taking some of the old stems right back to the base of the plant, and tie in the new growth. It's very easy to tell the old wood – darker, browner, with clusters of dead flowers – from the new wood – greener, with no flowers. When pruning vigorous ramblers, especially if they are growing up trees, do wear eye protection, because as you pull the old growths out, they could easily whip across your face and cause quite a painful injury.

Both rambling and climbing roses should be fed and watered well after pruning.

Dead-heading

All roses benefit from dead-heading – the removal of dead flower heads – unless you want to have rosehips to look at in the winter. Not only does the rose look neater without dead flowers on it, dead-heading prevents the plant putting all its energy into setting seed – the hips – and diverts it into producing more flowers this year or new growths for the following year. With roses that produce single blooms, snip the dead head off just above the first outward-facing leaf below it – usually the second or third down. This encourages that leaf bud to produce a new outward-facing shoot.

With roses that produce their flowers in clusters, you can snip out the blooms as they fade and then, when they have all faded, snip out the remains of the whole cluster, again to an outward-facing leaf. If you don't have time, just leave dead-heading till they have all faded.

Flowering shrubs

The key to pruning the most common flowering shrubs you're likely to find in your garden – flowering currant (*ribes*), lilac (*syringa*), mock orange (*philadelphus*), broom (*cytisus/genista*), bachelors' buttons (*kerria*), weigela, hardy fuchsia, butterfly bush (*buddleja*) – lies in knowing when they flower. Those that flower before midsummer, do so on the growth they made the previous summer. As soon as flowering has finished, you should prune the wood that has borne the flowers so that the shrub can put its energy for the rest of the summer into producing new growth for next year's flowers. In fact, with very early summer-flowering types like lilac

If it flowers before mid-June, prune after flowering. If it flowers after mid-June, prune in early spring

(*syringa*), you could even prune them while they are actually in flower – cutting bunches to bring indoors because it is usually too chilly in the garden at that time of year to get the benefit of their lovely scent outside!

These early-flowering shrubs don't need to be pruned every year, only when they get too big for their allotted space or they get so congested in the centre that a good clear out is in order. You can revitalize such shrubs by cutting them right back to a few centimetres above the ground in spring, and feeding them well. You won't get any flowers that year but you will get a much improved shrub that will flower better the following year. That will also happen if you prune by mistake in late winter or early spring.

Late summer-flowering shrubs like hardy fuchsias and the butterfly bush (*buddleja*), produce flowers only on growth made in the current year and so they must be pruned back hard – to the first buds of last year's growth – every spring. If you don't prune them, you get lots of gnarled, bare branches with just a few small leaves and flowers at the top.

Shrubs that are grown mainly for their foliage, like the golden elder (*sambucus*) or for their brightly coloured winter stems like the dogwood (*Cornus alba*), can also be pruned hard in the spring. Again, it is the new growth that produces the biggest and brightest leaves that summer or the most vividly coloured bark the following winter. Since these shrubs flower in early summer, pruning them hard in spring means that you will lose the flowers – but since they are far less attractive than the foliage or stems, it's not a hard choice.

Some shrubs, like purple-leafed varieties of the smoke bush (*Cotinus coggygria*), are grown for their tiny pinky-mauve flowers in early summer, which give the shrub its common name, as well as for their rich purple foliage. The best compromise here is to cut half the stems back hard in the spring to get the best foliage, and leave the rest to flower.

Left: Faith rewarded. By midsummer, the rose we had pruned so hard three months earlier was covered in flowers – larger, brighter and in greater numbers than before.

Inset: Dead-heading roses is a form of midsummer pruning and encourages the plant to keep on flowering.

Above and below: This dead nettle (Lamium maculatum 'Beacon Silver'), is an excellent ground-cover plant and one of the very few silver-leafed plants that will grow well in shade. By the middle of the summer, though, like some other ground-cover plants grown primarily for their foliage, it can start to look rather scruffy. Trimming off the dead flower stems and the tattiest-looking leaves with secateurs encourages the plant to produce a fresh new crop of bright silver foliage.

The following spring, cut out the other half and leave last year's new wood to flower. With deciduous shrubs, you don't need to make sloping cuts. Cut straight across the stem either just above a leaf or a bud if the plant is dormant or, if the leaves are arranged in pairs, between a pair of leaves.

Evergreens

Evergreen shrubs grown for their foliage really don't need any routine pruning except to remove any dead or diseased growth or when they outgrow their allotted space. With the laurel in the Square garden 'outgrow' was hardly the word. It was almost 6m (20ft) tall and about 4m (14ft) across – in a garden less than 10sq m (43sq ft). Radical solutions were called for. The owners were reluctant to take it out altogether because it screened the houses at the bottom of the garden. Pruning was the answer.

Luckily, laurels are extremely tolerant of hard pruning and it could have been taken back to 30–60cm (1–2ft) from the ground and would still have regrown. Since that would have left the garden rather exposed for a year or two, as a compromise, it was cut down to 1.8m (6ft), using telescopic loppers on the higher branches, a bow saw on the thicker ones (both from a hire shop) and secateurs on the thinner ones. With an evergreen which has large glossy leaves, using shears or an electric hedge trimmer isn't a good idea because, if you cut through the leaves, the remaining bits turn brown and look very ugly.

The best time to prune evergreens is in mid to late spring when the plant is just about to start into growth. The new growth will have the whole summer to ripen, ready to cope with the winter frosts. If you prune too early, you jump-start the shrub into premature growth that could be damaged by late frost or cold winds. If you prune too late, the new growth will still be soft and vulnerable to frost damage the following winter. By

> *Prune evergreens in spring, just as they start making new growth*

the end of the summer, the laurel in the Square garden had produced masses of new growth, completely hiding the cuts we had made, and adding at least 60cm (2ft) in height. We then pruned it again, very lightly, taking out about a third of the new growth.

Some common evergreen shrubs, like rose of Sharon (*Hypericum calycinum*) and *Mahonia aquifolium*, if they are grown as wide-spreading ground cover rather than as specimen shrubs, will actually benefit from being cut back almost to ground level each spring. Clip them over with shears after they've flowered to prevent them getting leggy and scruffy.

Clematis

When it comes to pruning, these lovely colourful climbers instil almost as much terror into new gardeners as roses. Again, it is a quite unnecessary panic. Admittedly, there are different groups which, in an ideal world, require slightly different treatment, but it is possible to prune clematis successfully by following a few simple guidelines.

The first group, the early (flowering at the beginning of summer) small-flowered types like *Clematis montana* need no pruning unless they have outgrown their allotted space. If your montana has got too big, wait until it has finished flowering and then cut it back with shears to well below the dimensions you want, bearing in mind it will grow again very quickly. Don't be nervous about cutting it back hard. I once tried to get rid of a huge montana by chopping it back to ground level, only to find it producing masses of healthy growth the following year! In fact, that is how to renovate an overgrown plant which will benefit from a severe haircut every five years or so.

The other spring-flowering clematis – the macropetalas and alpina, with small nodding flowers – are nothing like as vigorous. Nonetheless, they also benefit from an annual pruning after flowering, cutting the flowered growth back to about 30cm (1ft) from the main stems.

The second group – the large-flowered hybrids like 'Nellie Moser', that flower in midsummer (with perhaps a few more flowers later in the season) – are pruned along the same lines as early-summer flowering shrubs because, like them, they flower on growth produced in the previous year. So, immediately after flowering, cut back the side shoots that have borne flowers to within a few buds of the main framework. Don't cut out any of the new growth made in the current season because that will produce smaller flowers in late summer. The growth produced after you've pruned will carry the flowers the following year.

If you inherit a neglected clematis from this group, cut it back hard in the spring to the lowest pair of buds above ground level and feed it well. You will lose the flowers for the season after pruning but you will have a much healthier, bushier plant.

The third group includes all types which flower from midsummer onwards, including some large-flowered hybrids like 'Jackmanii', as well as the small-flowered *C. viticella* and *C. texensis* varieties. Like late summer-flowering shrubs, these produce flowers only on growth made in the current season. If you don't prune them, you will find you're looking at bare, unattractive stems on your wall or fence, while the flowers are blushing unseen on top of the wall. Cut all the dead growth back to the first pair of buds above ground level in late winter. These clematis are ideal for growing through shrubs, especially winter- or spring-flowering ones, because they provide extra colour at a different time of year. Since the clematis growth is cut away before the host shrub flowers, it doesn't interfere with it at all.

If you are planting a new clematis, be really brave. It is very hard for new gardeners to cut off healthy growth, but that's what you should do to

❛ With shrubs grown for flowers and foliage, prune half the stems hard back one year and the rest the following year to get the best of both worlds ❜

get a climber with lots of strong stems, rather than just one main one. If you plant in the autumn when the clematis is dormant, cut it back in winter to the lowest pair of strong buds. If you don't plant till spring or summer, allow it to grow and flower that season, then prune it back very hard the following winter. If it's in the first or second group, cut back half of the new growth to a pair of healthy buds but, if it's in the third group, cut it back to the lowest pair of healthy buds on each shoot.

Honeysuckle

There are two main types of honeysuckle (*lonicera*). One, like the summer-flowering evergreen Japanese honeysuckle (*Lonicera japonica*) produces its flowers on the current season's growth. It should be clipped over with shears in March or April as it starts into growth, just to keep it tidy. The other type includes the very popular early and late Dutch honeysuckle (*Lonicera periclymenum* 'Serotina' and 'Belgica') with larger, scented flowers – pink and cream, and crimson and cream respectively – borne on side shoots produced from the previous season's growth. This type should be trimmed immediately after flowering.

The ideal time to prune a neglected old honeysuckle is early spring for the first type or after flowering for the second. However, timing is not vital as you probably won't get many – if any – flowers the season after such a severe pruning.

To prune neglected honeysuckle, first untie it from its supports and, if possible, lay it flat on the ground. Untangle it, cutting out some of the oldest growths, either to the base or to just above a point where strong, young growth is emerging. Then tie the remaining growths to a support, fanning them out as evenly as possible.

Above: Sowing hardy annuals where they are to flower is one of the easiest ways of filling your borders in their first season. For the greatest impact, go for blocks of the same colour, like white Lavatera *'Mont Blanc', the pink variety 'Silver Cup' behind it, and the cornflowers (centaurea) to the right.*

Left: Once the seeds have germinated it is vital to thin them out to the proper distance otherwise you will wind up with weak, spindly seedlings, most of which will die, and the few survivors will never make good plants. An old table fork makes the perfect tool for lifting seedlings without damaging the roots.

GROWING YOUR OWN

Growing annuals is the cheapest, easiest and most colourful way of filling any gaps in a border or, where money is really tight, of creating a whole new border from scratch in just a few months.

There are two main types of annuals. First of all, there are the half-hardy annuals like lobelia and petunias that cannot survive a frost. For this reason, they must be raised under glass and can only be planted out in late spring or even early summer, depending on your local climate. You can buy them as small plants from the garden centre, rather than growing them yourself from seed, but don't be tempted to buy them too early in the year.

The second type are the hardy annuals which you sow straight into the soil. You can sow them in the spring or, in some cases, the preceding autumn, to get them off to a flying start the following year. For the longest display of flowers, make several sowings a couple of weeks apart. There are hundreds of varieties to choose from, but stick to those that are easy to grow, like nasturtiums (*tropaeolum*), cornflowers (*centaurea*), alyssum, love-in-a-mist (*Nigella damascena*), mallow (*lavatera*), Californian poppies (*Eschscholzia californica*) and the poached-egg plant (*Limnanthes douglasii*). Choosing mostly single colours gives you more control over your colour scheme, although the odd patch of mixed colours can look very effective, too.

As always, your first job is to prepare the soil well. Assuming that you have already improved it

Right: One of the best ways of marking out sowing areas is to use fine sand in a wine bottle. Make good-sized drifts, weaving in and out of each other to get the most natural effect. You can either broadcast the seed within them, or you can sow in drills – shallow parallel lines scratched on the soil. The advantage here is that when the seeds germinate it's very easy to tell them from weedlings, since the former are in straight lines and the latter aren't.

as necessary (see pages 29–31), just add just a little fertilizer — not too much or you'll get masses of leaves and few flowers — and rake it over, or break it down with the back of a fork, until it is as fine as you can get it. This is what gardeners call 'a fine tilth' and, ideally, it should be the texture of fine breadcrumbs – seeds are very small and don't stand much chance of germinating if they have huge lumps of soil on their heads. If your soil is heavy clay or silt, make seed drills (lines scraped in the soil) about 2.5cm (1in) deep and 2.5cm (1in) wide and fill them with seed compost before you sow. If the soil is very dry, water the area with a sprinkler for an hour or so, and leave sowing until the soil is moist and crumbly, but not sticky. If you leave watering until after sowing, you might wash the seeds down into the soil from whence they never return, or clump them together, especially if you are heavy handed with the watering can.

Given that blocks of colour make more of an impact than a dolly mixture effect, it's a good idea to mark out your soil before you sow, dividing planting areas according to the varieties of seed you intend to use. Irregular drifts look better than squares or blocks, especially if they weave into each other. An empty wine bottle filled with fine sand is a good means of marking out the soil. Before you sow, bear in mind the eventual height of the plants – there is little point in putting something 15cm (6in) behind something 1m (40in) tall.

How to sow

There is no doubt that the most common mistake new gardeners make with seeds is to sow them too deeply. A seed needs little more than twice its own depth of soil on top of it, so you need to cover it only very lightly. After all, nobody makes drills for weed seeds — they just land on the soil and germinate very nicely on their own.

How you sow depends on the seed in question. Large seeds like nasturtiums (*tropaeolum*) and sunflowers (*helianthus*) can be sown individually at the recommended distance apart given on the packet. As a safeguard, it is a good idea to sow two together,

in case one doesn't germinate. If they both germinate, pull out the weaker seedling of the two.

Other seeds can be sown in different ways. With a large area, you can broadcast them. Mix them in a bucket with a good quantity of seed compost and scatter handfuls on to the prepared soil. You can also sow them in drills — parallel lines scraped in the soil within the informal drift you have marked out. Check on the seed packet what the final distance between plants should be and make your drills accordingly. The big advantage of sowing this way is that weeds will be germinating in your border at the same time as your flowers and, since they don't grow in straight lines, it will be relatively easy to tell the weedlings from the seedlings. Don't worry that the flowers will look regimented. Once the seedlings have been thinned out, they will grow together to fill up their allotted space.

Tip the seed from the packet into your non-favoured hand, then sow it exceedingly thinly, a pinch at a time, along the drill. With pelleted seed, put two pellets at the recommended planting distance apart. Remember that you're aiming for one plant every 15–20cm (6–8in) so it's just a waste of money to sow too thickly. When you've finished sowing, cover the drills very lightly with soil. Stick in a label to remind you of what you've got where and, if you are troubled with cats, stick a few twigs into the soil or use a chemical repellant to stop them using it as a litter tray. If there's no rain for the first week or so, water the bed extremely carefully with the finest spray.

Thinning

Once the seedlings are 2.5cm (1in) or so in height, you must thin them out. I know this is one of the hardest things for new gardeners to do. You're so thrilled that you've got the seeds to germinate at all that you're extremely reluctant to pull any of them up and throw them away. But you must, otherwise they will become pathetic, spindly little plants — if they don't all collapse and die first. You can do it in two stages — thin them now to about 5cm (2in) apart and then repeat in a couple of weeks so they are at their recommended spacing. If there are any obvious gaps, use spare plants to fill them in.

If you sowed very meanly, it will be easier to thin out. Choose the strongest-looking seedling to keep and, placing two fingertips on the soil on either side of it to hold it steady, very carefully pull out its neighbours. If you have clumps of seedlings, it's probably not possible to isolate the strongest one in the same way. Instead, use an old table fork to lever up a small clump very carefully. Choose the strongest-looking seedling and, holding it by a seed leaf (one of the two round ones that appear first), gently extricate it from the rest. Don't under any circumstances touch its very delicate root system. Still holding it by the seed leaf, lower its roots into the hole left by the clump you've removed and very carefully press soil around them to hold the seedling in place.

At the end of the season, dig or pull the annuals out. Many, such as alyssum, Californian poppies (*Eschscholzia californica*), love-in-a-mist (*Nigella damascena*), nasturtiums (*tropaeolum*) and the poached-egg plant (*Limnanthes douglasii*), self-seed (drop their seeds on to the soil where they germinate unaided) so, once you've sown them, you'll always have them. Just remember what the seedlings look like and avoid them when you're weeding.

Half-hardy annuals

Although growing half-hardy annuals is something you probably won't want to bother with as a new gardener, I would make an exception for a very

---

Six good hardy annuals for a sunny border

Alyssum

Cornflower (*centaurea*)

California poppy (*Eschscholzia californica*)

Lavatera trimestris 'Silver Cup'

Love-in-a-mist (*Nigella damascena*)

Poached-egg plant (*Limnanthes douglasii*)

Four good annuals for shade

Busy lizzie (*impatiens*)

Lobelia

Begonia

Monkey flower (*mimulus*)

---

useful group of annuals — climbers like morning glory (*ipomoea*), the cup-and-saucer vine (*Cobaea scandens*) and canary creeper (*Tropaeolum pelegrinum*), which are marvellous for covering fences and pergolas in a season. Since you need only a few plants, it is quite possible simply to raise them on a windowsill.

There are special discs available at garden centres that swell up once wet, forming the pot and the compost all in one. Alternatively, use well moistened peat pots filled with seed compost. In both instances, plant out the whole thing — the pots just break down in the soil, so you don't have to worry about taking the young plant out of a plastic pot and possibly damaging its roots in the process. Push a seed into the middle of each pot so that it's just covered with compost. Stand the pots in a plastic food box or empty ice-cream container, cover the top with clingfilm and put it in the airing cupboard, on the second or third shelf up. Check every day for the first shoots and when they appear, remove the clingfilm and stand the pots in a shallow tray on a sunny windowsill. Make sure the compost never dries out — pouring water into the tray and letting the compost suck it up is the easiest, most efficient method — and turn the tray daily to keep the seedlings growing upright rather than leaning towards the light.

Alternatively, make yourself a very simple light-reflecting box. Cut the front out of a large cardboard box and line the back and sides with foil or paint it with white gloss to reflect light all round the plants. This will keep them bushy and prevent them becoming drawn and leggy. Wait until all danger of frost is past before you plant them out.

PLANTS FOR FREE

Although I firmly believe that plants represent wonderful value for money – what else would give you as much pleasure for the same price as a rose – there's no doubt that when you need lots of them to fill a border, they do seem expensive. So any means of stretching the budget by getting plants for free, or almost, is well worth exploring.

Obviously, friends, relations and neighbours are a good source of cuttings or small plants, but if the plants you've set your heart on don't materialize, there are other ways.

One method is to buy a large perennial in a pot and divide it into several smaller plants. By the end of the summer, the new plants will cover a larger area than a single big plant could have done. The method of division you use depends on the plant. With plants that have fibrous roots, like lady's mantle (*Alchemilla mollis*), you should be able to pull them apart with your hands, dividing them into three or four smaller plants, each with plenty of roots. If you already have a clump growing in the garden, the same principle applies. Dig it up and shake off as much of the soil as you can. You'll probably find that the roots of larger perennials like Michaelmas daisies (*Aster novae-belgii*) are just too

Left: There may well be shrubs in your garden that will have to go, not because there's anything intrinsically wrong with them but because they don't fit in with your plans, they're too big or just in the wrong place. It makes sense to save them if you can and give them to someone else for free. The aim is to disturb the roots as little as possible, so dig out as big a ball of soil as possible, wrap it in polythene to stop the roots drying out, and get it into its new home as soon you can. If you trim off some of the top growth so that the plant can put its energies into making new roots and keep it well watered, it should survive.

Above: It's very easy to turn one large perennial, such as a hosta, into several smaller ones. In early spring, just as they are producing new leaves, saw the plant into pieces with an old bread knife, making sure that each has a shoot and a good share of root.

Left: With plants that have masses of thread-like roots, such as lady's mantle (Alchemilla mollis), you should be able to work your thumbs into the plant's rootball and pull it into several pieces. As long as each new plant has a good clump of roots, it should settle in and start to grow very quickly.

Above: When you're clearing out a weed-infested patch in the garden, you may well find there are some decent plants underneath that are well worth saving. Be sure to clean them up thoroughly first, removing all trace of weeds and their roots before replanting.

tough and tangled to be pulled apart. The classic method of separating them is to put two garden forks back to back in the centre of the clump (yes, I know. Borrow one from a neighbour in return for a few of the divisions) and then lever it apart. Repeat until the clumps are small enough to separate by hand. Keep the younger, more vigorous growth from the outside of the clump and put the old, woody, central bit on the compost heap.

Plants with fleshy roots, like hostas or lupins (*lupinus*), need sawing into pieces with something like an old bread knife. Ideally, do it in spring when the plant has just started into growth, so you can make sure each piece has some leaf buds, or the beginnings of new leaves, and some root. Hostas, in particular, dislike being disturbed so they may not look great in the first season after division, but they will romp away soon after.

Cutting costs

Taking cuttings may sound like real grown-up gardening, but with some shrubs like dogwood (*Cornus alba*) and the butterfly bush (*buddleja*), it's really easy and, since you're bound to know someone who has a suitable parent shrub, it makes sense to have a go at least. Rosemary (*rosmarinus*) and lavender (*lavendula*) also root very easily in summer so by taking cuttings from your own plants you could have a whole rosemary or lavender hedge for free within a year or two.

Pull off pieces of new growth about 10–15cm (4–6in) long that haven't borne flowers, trim them cleanly across the bottom, taking off the jagged 'heel' of bark, and remove the lower leaves. Push most of each bare stem into a pot of compost – four cuttings to a 10-cm (4-in) pot – making sure the leaves clear the surface. Cover with a polythene bag. Leave them outside until they have rooted – new growth at the top indicates that they have. Put each one carefully into its own pot and

Gardeners are very generous, but always ask before you take cuttings

keep it somewhere light but sheltered until the spring, then plant it out.

Saving money

Summer bedding plants are expensive as they usually last one season, but you can save money by overwintering the more expensive half-hardy perennials in your containers – geraniums (*pelargonium*), fuchsias, etc – in a cool, frost-free place.

In early autumn, dismantle your containers, carefully removing the plants you're going to save. Shake off surplus compost, trim the top growth to about 10cm (4in), remove all leaves, and trim the roots to about 5cm (2in). Half-fill a 10-cm (4-cm) plastic pot with compost, put in the plant and then fill it with compost. Water the pots well, leave them to drain, then stand them in a light but frost-free place – an unheated porch or even a spare bedroom with the central heating turned off. You shouldn't have to water them again all winter unless the compost becomes very dry, and then you should water them only very sparingly.

When the new shoots appear in early spring, water them more regularly and once the plants are growing well give them a liquid feed once a week. Plant them out in late spring when all danger of frost is past.

You can save tuberous begonias, too. Remove them from the compost and leave them for a week or so to dry out. Then trim away all the top growth and the roots, and dust the tubers with fungicide. Fill a shallow tray with dry silver sand or dry peat substitute and bury them in it, spaced well apart. Store them in a cool, dry, frost-free place. In spring, put them hollow-side up in pots of moist compost and stand them in a light, frost-free place. Once they are producing new growth, feed them once a week and plant them out in late spring/early summer.

Busy lizzies (*impatiens*), which are quite tricky to grow from seed, are exceptionally easy to grow from cuttings. Buy one decent-sized plant, and turn it into eight or ten! In early summer, simply cut 4–7 cm (2–3 in) off the tip of a young shoot that hasn't yet flowered, trim it with a sharp knife and stand it in water. The easiest way is to take a jam jar filled with water, place a piece of fairly stiff paper across the top and fix it round the neck with an elastic band. Then cut one small hole in the paper for each cutting and push it through so that the stem is in the water, but the leaves are resting on the paper. Once the cuttings have formed a good, solid clump of roots, pot them up in soil-less potting compost. You can start them off in potting compost right away, but I think the water method is easier.

❛ Save even more money by overwintering geraniums and fuchsias and taking cuttings in spring ❜

We used spider plants (*chlorophytum*) in our baskets. As they produce lots of babies it is easy to increase your stock. Either remove a well developed plantlet from its parent by the same technique as for busy lizzies (*impatiens*) or leave them attached to their parents and push the base of the plantlet into a pot of moist compost. Once rooted, cut the umbilical cord.

Free gifts

If there are shrubs in your garden that you don't want, dig them out and give them to someone else for free. Since you're going to get rid of them anyway, it's always worth trying to save them. It's possible with many plants because they are shallow-rooted, but others, like roses, which have one main, deep tap root, tend not to transplant very well once they are more than a few years old.

Late winter/early spring is a good time to do it because they're about to start into growth and so will establish themselves more quickly. In the case of a winter-flowering shrub like jasmine (*jasminum*), it makes sense to prune it back quite hard before you move it so that the shrub can put all its energies into making new roots rather than wasting

it on flowers and setting seed. The less you disturb the roots, the better a shrub will establish itself, so dig out as big a ball of soil around the roots – called the rootball – as practical. As a rough guide, the roots will extend about as far as the canopy of top growth, though it won't matter if you lose some of the very fine ones at the edges.

Then take a sheet of heavy duty polythene and roll up half of its width. Push the shrub away from you, tilting the rootball backwards, then slide the polythene, rolled-up section first, underneath it. Next, pull the shrub towards you, rocking the rootball forwards onto the flat part of the polythene and then unroll the other part, so that the shrub is sitting in the centre. Wrap it around the rootball and tie it round the main stem before you lift it out. Ideally, the hole for it should be pre-dug so that it spends as little time out of the ground as possible. Make sure that the shrub gets lots of water until it has re-established. The appearance of new growth will tell you that it has.

If you are clearing a weed-infested area, it's possible to save plants buried underneath and use them elsewhere in the garden, providing you remove all traces of weeds first. The last thing you want to do is re-import into your nice clean soil all those weeds you've struggled to eliminate.

Carefully dig up the plant with a good-sized rootball, and pull any obvious weeds out of the clump. Shake off as much soil as you can and look at the roots. It's not hard to work out which belong to the plant – they're in the majority and are firmly attached. Everything else should be carefully teased out and disposed of. Replant it right away in its new position if you can. If not, and you've got lots of plants, dig a trench in an out-of-the-way corner and plant them there for the time being. If it's just a couple, put them in pots until you're ready to plant them out. In the Square garden, we saved a small piece of London pride (*saxifraga*), and finally replanted it in the gravel bed by the pond.

PORTABLE GARDENS

If you have nothing but a concrete yard, a balcony or a flat roof, how can you still make the space infinitely more attractive and get a great deal of pleasure from it? The answer is growing plants in containers. Lots of new gardeners are mobile, living in short-term accommodation where they know they're not going to be staying long and so they are reluctant to spend time and money on the garden. Growing plants in containers means that your garden is portable.

Even if you have a garden and intend to stay put, containers are still invaluable. They will cheer up difficult, soil-less corners and enable you to grow plants that wouldn't thrive in your soil or would not be hardy enough to survive the winter outside. They are especially useful in small gardens where you can ring the changes through the seasons, bringing containers to the fore when the plants are at their best and moving them to a less prominent position afterwards.

Choosing your container

The range of containers available now is vast – from the purpose-made and expensive to the improvised, cheap and cheerful. Your choice will depend largely on the state of your bank balance and the style of your garden. Grand stone urns look a bit silly in small suburban gardens, while bright plastic in simple shapes looks best in a modern urban setting. The one feature that is absolutely essential in any container is good drainage holes in the bottom. Without them, the compost becomes waterlogged and stale and the plants will die.

TERRACOTTA
There is no doubt that handmade terracotta is the ultimate. It starts off looking wonderful and gets even better as it ages. Unfortunately, it's also very expensive. Terracotta is also breakable and can flake or crack if it freezes, so choose containers that are guaranteed frost-proof. (The guarantee doesn't mean they won't crack – just that you'll get your money back if they do!) The other problem with

Above: An attractive, cool combination of silver, cream, pale green and purple with variegated sage, trailing helichrysum and osteospermums.

Right: A patio herb garden in containers is both useful and decorative. The white-flowered plant in front, bacopa, is not a herb, but shows the effectiveness of a container filled with just one plant.

Below: Drill holes in plastic pots to ensure good drainage.

terracotta is that they lose water quickly because they are porous, though a lining of black polythene will help keep in moisture.

MACHINE-MADE TERRACOTTA

This is the cheaper version of terracotta, coming in a narrower range of simpler shapes. It's a bit bright when new, but a coat of well-thinned white emulsion will give it an instant weathered look.

TERRAPERMA

This is 'plastic terracotta' and it looks just like the real thing. Normally, I don't like fakes, but I make an exception for these. It is cheap – a big pot costs a fraction of the price of the real thing – it's virtually indestructible and it's very light. This is a definite plus where weight is a major consideration – on balconies or roof gardens. The one drawback is that it doesn't weather like the real thing, so you will need to grow plants like ivy to trail over the edges. You'll also need to punch or drill out the moulded drainage holes in the bottom before you plant as they are sold unpunched for indoor use.

RECONSTITUTED STONE

These are modelled on antique stone urns and bowls and while they are much cheaper than the real thing – I won't even talk about the real thing because I'm sure if you had that kind of money to spend, you'd rather have a car – they are still pricey. They look rather bright when they are new but they will soon weather down, especially if you paint them with plain yogurt, sour milk, or even liquid manure, all of which encourage lichen and algae to grow.

CEMENT

This is the cheap version of reconstituted stone but, if you choose carefully and go for good, simple shapes, giving them the old yogurt/sour milk/liquid manure treatment, they soon look good.

GLAZED POTS

These lovely coloured pots from China have recently become very popular. They are frost proof and in the medium price range. They come in plain colours, like stone, deep blue or a paler blue-green like the one we used in the City garden. They also come decorated with a crackled effect, painted with flowers or with a bamboo design etched into the glaze.

WOOD

Wood is a good material for containers and comes in a variety of forms. At the posh end there are Versailles tubs, square with balls on each corner. These look stunning in a formal setting – either side of a door, for example. They need re-painting every three years or so, so buy a plastic pot to fit inside which can be lifted out easily.

HALF BARRELS

The real McCoy are made from oak and half barrels are a chunkier, cheaper wooden option. Treat them with a wood preservative to prevent rotting and leave them to weather to an attractive silvery-brown. Alternatively, you can stain them with a coloured woodstain, as we did in the City garden. With a bit of care, they should last a good few years.

You can also buy specially made half barrels, usually made from hardwood. These are quite expensive, but they will last for years without treatment. They are usually varnished so they stay a rather obtrusive glossy chestnut colour which is a shame. For a cottage garden, there are rustic effect ones too – square tubs and troughs made of rough sawn timber or logs.

PLASTIC

There are some excellent plastic containers around now in a range of finishes – shiny, matt or textured – and colours such as white, brown, stone, terracotta and any number of greens. They work best when they are not pretending to be anything else and are particularly good in a modern garden where it's going to be most appropriate to have simple shapes like flowerpots or tubs.

IMPROVISED CONTAINERS

There are many good plastic containers around now, designed for use indoors, but by making drainage holes in the bottom you can transform them for garden use. If you have a drill, use the largest bit you have to make a series of linked holes around the centre until eventually it turns into one decent-sized hole. If you don't have a drill, you could use – with extreme care – a red-hot skewer to do the same thing. Always aim for a good sized drainage hole. Lots of tiny holes will just clog up with compost.

We bought very elegant, dirt cheap Swedish wastepaper baskets at a chain store and sprayed them a sludgy grey-green with Kolorbond (a product designed for the building trade to spray UVP windowframes a whole range of colours). Depending on the type of plastic you're painting, you may have to use a special primer first.

Brightly coloured plastic dustbins can look very good in an inner city backyard. Use them for a small tree, a large shrub or even runner beans growing up a wigwam of canes.

METAL CONTAINERS
Galvanized buckets and oval mop buckets make good containers, too, especially after the bright silver colour has mellowed to a more leaden grey. You can also buy galvanized florists' buckets, which are tall and slender without a handle.

A really cheap alternative is to use very large catering tins (a local restaurant, café or canteen might be willing to save you some) and paint them with exterior gloss paint. Painting them all the same colour will give the group a pleasing unity, especially if you've got a variety of different sizes.

Be eclectic. You can use an old tin bath, an old watering can – anything that appeals.

BASKETS
These come in a whole range of shapes and sizes, and you get a lot of container for your money. They won't last forever, of course, but they will give you quite a few years' service if you paint them first with three coats of waterproof polyurethane yacht varnish.

❛ Put in a 'crocking layer' – polystyrene bits will do – to aid drainage ❜

Before you plant, place a layer of small plastic flowerpots, upside down, in the bottom. Line the basket with thick black polythene and make slits in the bottom for drainage. The flowerpots will keep the wet polythene off the bottom of the basket and prevent it rotting too quickly.

TEA CHESTS
These make another useful, short-term container for a small tree or large shrub. Paint it first with yacht varnish or exterior gloss. If you are a dab hand with a brush or a stencil you could even add a few decorative flourishes.

CERAMICS
Old ceramic sinks make good troughs for alpines, though they look better if you coat them first with hypertufa. This is a mixture of two parts coir to one part coarse sand and one part cement, mixed to a thick paste with water.

Before you apply the hypertufa, score the surface of the sink and give it a coat of a bonding agent like Unibond. Wearing gloves, apply the hypertufa by hand about 2cm (³/₄in) thick and leave the surface rough. It looks a bit more like stone that way and if you want to encourage lichen and algae, they prefer a rough surface.

UNLIKELY CONTAINERS
Some people even plant up old lavatory pans, but they must be round the bend. Others grow plants in margarine tubs, coffee jars, old freezer trays or polystyrene boxes. While you certainly can grow plants in almost anything, containers like this do little for the attractiveness of your garden.

How to plant up a container

Once it's full of compost, a very large container will be too heavy to move. So, before planting, the first job is to move it into its permanent position. Put in a layer of crocks to keep the compost away from

Above: In the City garden, the Tumbler tomato plants cropped for a couple of months and produced more tomatoes than Catherine's family could eat.

Near right: We planted herbs in old apple boxes, stained blue to match the other woodwork in the garden. They were then lined with polythene, and slits were cut in for drainage.

Centre right: One of the boxes was stacked on top of the others, to give some height to the arrangement.

Far right: Golden variegated ginger mint, green and white pineapple mint, as well as plain spearmint, look as good as they taste.

the drainage hole and allow water to drain through. People used to use bits of broken terracotta flower-pots, but that's not an option any more. Broken-up polystyrene packaging is a good substitute. It's light, free, and doesn't break down. It should fill the bottom fifth of the pot. You can put in more if you're growing shallow-rooted plants.

If you want to plant trees or shrubs in a permanent container, you will need a soil-based potting compost like John Innes No. 3. Fill the container to just below the depth of the largest plant's existing pot. Take the plant out of its pot, setting it on the compost and arranging the other plants around it. Fill in the gaps with compost. Alternatively, you can fill the container to the top with compost, then dig the planting holes.

The key to success with container gardening is proper feeding and watering. Since the limited amount of compost in the container can't provide all the food and water the plant needs, you must ensure it has plenty of both. There will be enough nutrients in the compost for the first few weeks, but you will have to water every day in summer even when it rains. The surface area of compost is too small to collect anything like the amount of water needed and, as the plants grow, they form an effective umbrella against the rain. Adding water-retaining gel crystals to the compost helps. These swell up to hold many hundreds of times their own weight in water which they then release slowly into the compost. But regular, copious watering – until it starts running out of the bottom of the pot – is what's needed.

Although the compost contains some nutrients, you can add controlled-release fertilizer as you plant, either as granules or plugs. Permanent plants will need feeding thereafter every spring. After the first couple of years, you should carefully scrape off the top layer of the old compost and replace it with new.

With annuals, if you haven't used controlled-release fertilizer, feed them every week with liquid tomato fertilizer or special liquid feed. To keep them flowering all summer long, dead-head regularly, every few days. If dead flowers are allowed to develop into seed pods, the plant thinks it has succeeded in reproducing itself and so stops flowering. Foliage plants like silvery helichrysum can get leggy and scruffy, but if you prune them back hard to new growth, they'll produce a fresh crop of leaves. You can cut back trailing petunias, too, and get a second or even third flush of flowers.

What to grow

Although most people tend to grow bedding plants in their containers, you can, in fact, grow virtually anything you like – even trees! Obviously you will need a large pot at least 45cm (18in) in both diameter and depth and only a small tree although, since its roots will be confined in the container, it will only reach a fraction of its potential size. Some of the small flowering cherries like *Prunus* 'Accolade' or a crab apple like Sargent's crab (*Malus sargentii*) would be good, as would Japanese maples (*Acer japonicum*), and weeping trees like the small Kilmarnock willow (*Salix caprea pendula*). You could try fruit trees – apples or cherries grown on a dwarfing rootstock to keep them small, or Ballerina apples – specially bred as slender single-stemmed small trees. You'll need two different varieties which flower at the same time to pollinate each other.

Conifers can make very good container plants in a formal setting – flanking a flight of steps for example. Look for something like a dwarf Lawson's cypress (*Chamaecyparis lawsoniana* 'Ellwoodii'), or a juniper like *J. communis* 'Hibernica' or even yew – which is not as slow growing as people think. Underplanted with bulbs for spring and bedding in summer, they look very striking.

Patio roses have been specially bred for this purpose and new ones are being introduced all the time. Look for the warm pink 'Gentle Touch', the soft yellow 'House Beautiful', the rosy pink 'Queen

> *Water thoroughly every day – twice in very hot weather*

Mother' (though make sure you get the patio rose, not the much larger floribunda of the same name) or, if you love bright colours, the vivid vermilion 'Top Marks'.

Small shrubs are also ideal for containers, though it makes sense to choose those with the longest possible flowering season. Potentillas are hard to beat, with masses of small open-faced flowers all summer long. They come in a wide range of colours now from brick red through pinks and oranges to yellows and whites. There are lots of good varieties around, but look for *P. fruticosa* 'Abbotswood' with its pure white flowers and grey-green foliage, the soft primrose *P. f.* 'Primrose Beauty' and the peachy-coloured *P. f.* 'Day Dawn'. Hebes are also a good bet here. Most flower slightly later, from midsummer into the autumn and have the plus of evergreen leaves which often take on an attractive wine-red flush in autumn. Look for 'Marjorie', 'Midsummer Beauty' and 'Autumn Glory'.

You can grow climbers, too, either up a wall or free-standing with their own built-in support. The simplest and cheapest support is a wigwam of bamboo canes or hazel poles. For something more ornamental, you can now buy products like the 'Cocoon' which has thin slats of wood bellying out from tight rings top and bottom, rather like a Chinese lantern. Left plain, or stained with a coloured wood stain, it makes an instant feature even before it's planted up. You could grow one of the less vigorous clematis up it – one of the spring-flowering alpinas perhaps, or the later-flowering 'Gravetye Beauty' – provided you can keep the roots cool, or a passion flower (*passiflora*) – again, ideally one of the less vigorous kinds, like the white 'Constance Elliott'. Annual climbers like morning glories (*ipomoea*), canary creeper (*Tropaeum peregrinum*), or sweet peas (*Lathyrus odoratus*) would also be good, though the latter are very greedy feeders so add some good rich organic matter to the compost before you plant.

Plants in containers are slightly more vulnerable

> ❝ *Feed containers and baskets once a week* ❞

to damage from the cold than the same plants growing in a border. A small, isolated amount of compost above ground can freeze more easily than the soil in your garden. In winter, wrap a few layers of sacking, loft insulating material (inside a black plastic bag to keep it dry) or garden fleece round pots for protection in a very cold snap.

Hanging baskets

Everyone has room for a hanging basket somewhere and they are a wonderful, quick and relatively cheap way of livening up the dullest walls with living colour. Go for the biggest basket you can manage because they look so spectacular – 35cm (14in) is fine, 40cm (16in) is even better if you have the space. The best baskets are plastic-coated wire ones. You can plant into their sides and get a wonderful ball of colour. Ideally, the baskets should have easily removable chains.

Set your empty basket on a bucket or large flowerpot and line it. You can use sphagnum moss (grown specially for the purpose, not taken from the wild) which you buy in bags from garden centres. Tease it out to cover the sides and leave a good thick collar at the top, coming well above the rim of the basket to prevent water pouring out. To stop the water draining through too fast, put in an old plastic saucer or circle of polythene with a few slits in the bottom of the basket.

For a new gardener, a coir matting liner would be simpler. You can cut it so you can still plant through the sides of the basket and once the plants start growing you don't see it. Get the size bigger than your basket so it stands proud of the rim. You can trim it at the end and, later, you can re-use it.

Next, put a shallow layer of compost in the bottom. A lighter peat or, preferably, coir-based compost is fine – the plants are only in it for one season and weight is a factor. Add some water-retaining gel crystals.

Left: Hanging baskets can brighten up any wall, sunny or shady, as long as you choose the right plants for the conditions. Geraniums, osteospermums and kingfisher daisies, for example, all need plenty of sun to do well, whereas fuchsias, begonias, and busy lizzies will all thrive in shade, while lobelia will be happy in both. Don't forget that some houseplants, like the spider plant and tradescantia will grow outside during the summer, giving welcome greenery and interesting foliage shapes to a basket. Since most baskets are seen from below, choose plenty of trailing plants to hang down, as well as upright ones for the centre of the basket.

Above: Support the basket on a bucket or large flower pot as you work. Line it with a coir lining and a circle of polythene with a few cuts in it for drainage.
Left: Make slits in the sides of the coir liner for the lobelia, making some higher, some lower to get better coverage.
Below left: Very gently squeeze the rootball of each lobelia into a flattened sausage shape and carefully work it through the slit in the liner. Cover the roots with compost.
Below right: Place the remaining plants, still in their pots, in the basket, and move them around until you are happy that you have got the most attractive arrangement. Then plant them, filling in the gaps with compost.

If you are using lobelia in the basket, remove one plug from its module, very carefully compress the roots and, having made a small hole in the moss or cut a slit in the coir matting, slide the rootball carefully through. Put two or three plants evenly spaced between the second and third wires, and another two or three between the third and the fourth to give you a staggered effect and the best coverage. Cover the roots with more compost.

Arrange the rest of your plants, still in their pots, in the basket and play with them. To give the basket height, you want a tall plant in the centre and some trailing ones near the edge. When you're happy with the arrangement, take the plants out of their pots, position them in the basket and fill in the gaps with compost. Leave a good two or three centimetres clear at the top of the basket so that you don't get composty water splashing out.

If you use a coir fibre liner, choose the size bigger than your basket and trim it after planting

Plants for a hanging basket

What you choose will depend to a degree on whether the baskets are in sun or shade. In a sunny spot, you can grow all the traditional bedding plants, like geraniums (*pelargonium*), petunias, verbena and newer ones like the pretty blue kingfisher daisy (*felicia*). In shade, the choice is more restricted but, fortunately, there are lots of lovely plants like fuchsias, begonias, busy lizzies (*impatiens*) and lobelia that do very well.

Foliage is as important as flowers in all hanging baskets. Foliage plants like silvery helichrysum, ivy (*hedera*) and glechoma are all good, and don't forget that houseplants like spider plants or tradescantia will thrive outside in the summer.

The minimum number of plants for a good display in a 35cm (14in) basket is one tall central plant, three foliage plants, three trailing flowering plants, six other flowering plants and a strip (10 or 12 small plants) of lobelia.

As for colour, the choice is endless. Baskets with all the colours of the rainbow can work well, but some of the most memorable baskets stick to just a few colours. Blue, pink, white and silver is a popular combination, giving a soft cottagey effect, blue white and yellow is crisp and modern-looking, while that good old patriotic standby red, white and blue always looks very striking. Our baskets in the Oblong garden for example were white, deep orange and blue, with white fuchsias and busy lizzies, deep orange mimulus and trailing begonias, pale blue lobelia and cool cream and green spider plants. Baskets of a single colour can be stunning. Just think of an all-white basket in a part-shaded spot – trailing ivy-leafed geraniums, regal pelargoniums, large-flowered tuberous begonias, white lobelia, or an all-yellow one, ranging from deep cream through lemon, butter and sunshine to deep gold. Baskets of just one type of plant can also be extremely eye-catching. You must have seen those huge globes of trailing Surfinia petunias in deep magenta or pale lavender blue with which the front of every pub in the land seems to have been bedecked these last few summers!

You don't have to stick to summer bedding in your baskets. You could grow miniature roses, herbs, tomatoes – 'Tumbler' would be perfect – and even trailing strawberries. The slugs wouldn't get them, though the birds might have a field day!

Don't think that baskets are only a summer feature. In the winter they can provide even more welcome colour. Use small-leafed variegated ivies as trailing plants and fill in with colourful winter-flowering pansies. Plant a few bulbs like crocuses for a spring bonus.

Taking care of your baskets

With baskets more than any other container, the key to success is how you look after them. Once the plants start to grow, the compost is just a mass of tiny roots fighting for moisture and nutrients, and you have to provide it all. Baskets need soaking every day in summer – twice a day, if not three times, when it's hot and dry. Water slowly until it starts to drain from the bottom of the basket. If you have not put in some controlled-release fertilizer plugs, give them a liquid feed with tomato fertilizer or special container fertilizer every week.

Dead-head regularly, to encourage re-flowering. If you can be bothered, dead-head lobelia with nail scissors every few days but, if you think life's too short, chop it back fortnightly or so when it starts to look straggly. A little extra feed after you've chopped will get them going again quickly.

We did an experiment in our Oblong garden with a pair of identical baskets. One was fed and watered properly. The other was treated like all too many hanging baskets – given a milk-bottleful of water when the owner remembered, never fed or dead-headed. Within a couple of weeks, the difference in size was marked and, after a couple of months of hot weather, the neglected basket was half-dead, though the fuchsia and the begonias actually looked far better than expected. The well-tended basket was fine although, despite all the TLC lavished on it, weeks of exceptionally hot, dry air meant it wasn't as big as it would normally have been by that time.

At the end of summer, and before the first frosts, it's worth saving some of the plants for next year.

Vegetables

You can also grow some very easy vegetables and herbs in containers. We used lovely old wooden apple boxes with the price 5/- on the side, giving some indication of their age. We stained them with Lupine wood stain to match the other wood in the City garden and lined them with stout polythene,

> *Put an old plastic saucer or circle of polythene in the bottom to stop water draining through baskets too quickly*

with a few slits in the bottom for drainage. Some crops, like lettuce and rocket, don't need a great depth of soil, so put in a generous layer of broken-up polystyrene and a shallow layer of a soil-based compost on top. Sow the seed very thinly, one row every couple of weeks to ensure a succession of crops. Once they have germinated, thin them with a table fork so you have about four plants per row.

We sowed a cut-and-come-again salad bowl type lettuce, from which you can pick as many leaves as you need and leave the plant growing to produce more. Other crops, such as tomatoes, runner beans and even new potatoes, need a greater depth of soil and one with a lot of guts to it since they are very greedy feeders – try them in a plastic dustbin with drainage holes punched in the bottom. They also need masses of water, so the soil must be very water retentive. Mixing roughly equal quantities of soil-based compost and a manure-based product should give you the richness you need. Fill the boxes to within a few centimetres of the top.

If you want to try growing a few new potatoes, set out two seed potatoes in late spring, on about 15cm (6in) of compost and just cover them. As soon as leaves start to appear, add more compost, covering them again. Carry on until the compost is a few centimetres below the top of the container. This is called 'earthing up' and in theory you should get a cluster of potatoes for each time you've earthed them up. With runner beans, tomatoes and courgettes, you need to wait until all danger of frost is past. For runner beans, put one 1.8m (6ft) bamboo cane in each corner of the box and fix the canes together at the top. Put one plant in each corner and start it twining round the cane.

The best tomato for container gardening is 'Tumbler'. It produces lots of small sweet fruit from midsummer on. We underplanted them with purple basil – tomato salad in a box! Runner beans and tomatoes need feeding with tomato fertilizer once a week and watering daily – twice a day if it's hot.

GARDEN FEATURES

While you could think of features like water, lighting, seating and dining areas, and so on as the finishing touches, or the accessories, they are in fact crucial for getting the maximum enjoyment out of your garden.

Water in particular adds another dimension to any garden. Apart from the fact that it attracts wildlife, the sight of it gives you an endlessly changing show of reflections from the sky, the sound of it gently trickling or splashing is very relaxing and the idea of it takes your mind out of the garden. It may be only a small amount of water but its depths could be infinite.

There is no garden too small to have some kind of water feature. In our City garden, there wasn't room for a pond and besides, with a toddler in the house, safety considerations ruled it out. Instead, we created a very simple water feature, using a low-voltage, and therefore completely safe, DIY submersible pump, a wall mask and a reservoir tank. The tank is hidden beneath two paving slabs,

Left and far right: Using hoops and extensions in a simple pattern to make a back for the arbour not only looks attractive but provides support for climbers.

Above: Creating attractive seating areas in the garden is most important for getting maximum enjoyment out of it. Think about when you are most likely to be in the garden and choose the most suitable site. If you're out at work all day, for example, select a spot that gets the best of the evening sun. Scented plants are important near a seating area. We chose white roses ('Climbing Iceberg'), *which have a good perfume, and behind the bench, we also added sweetly scented tobacco plants (Nicotiana affinis) which are at their most fragrant in the evening. Underneath the bench and growing up through it, we planted lavender (lavendula) which releases its fragrance when its leaves are bruised, as they would be every time you sat down.*

angled very slightly towards the narrow central gap so that the water splashing onto them runs back into the tank below. To make sure the bulk of the water did run back in and didn't soak away into the surrounding soil, we used a sheet of butyl pond liner underneath the slabs, with a cross cut in it over the tank and with the resulting flaps stuck down against the sides with waterproof tape.

There are lots of different wall masks available now. We chose a ceramic one of a sun face in a blue-green glaze to tone with the woodwork in the garden. Rather than chase out a channel on the brick wall to take the feeder pipe, we made life simple by using flexible clear plastic tubing. Since the mask was set between two trellis diamonds, we ran the tubing along the underside of the trellis. The ivy planted underneath would soon grow up to cover the exposed pipe between the trellis and the mask.

The tank was simply filled up with a hose. In hot weather, when water evaporates very quickly, it needed topping up regularly. In autumn, it's recommended by the manufacturers that you take out the pump, dry it and store it indoors for the winter. When we did this in the City garden, we were surprised to discover a large and very healthy frog living in the tank.

Another good idea for an attractive, safe and simple water feature is a bubble jet pool, with water bubbling up through pebbles. You will need a pump with a special bubble jet nozzle, a reservoir tank buried in the ground and a sheet of stout, galvanized metal mesh strong enough to take not just the weight of the pebbles, but of a person, just in case someone steps on it by accident. Place the mesh over the reservoir, allowing an overlap of at least 30cm (12in) on each side. Then cover it with the most attractive pebbles you can find. The combination of the gentle burbling sound of the water and the wet, shiny surfaces of the pebbles makes it a very soothing feature.

> *It's perfectly safe to fit low-voltage DIY pumps and lighting yourself. For anything else, employ a professional electrician*

For something a little more elaborate, try laying a terracotta jar on its side with the water trickling out over its lip, onto the pebbles and back into the tank. It's actually much simpler to make than it looks. All you do is make a hollow in the soil to take the terracotta jar, placing it so that the bottom of the lip is slightly lower than the hole in the bottom of the pot. When you're happy with the position of the pot, firm the soil around it to keep it stable. Then fix some thin, transparent tubing to the pump, long enough to reach into the bottom of the pot. Block up the hole to keep the tubing in place with waterproof stopping such as plumberfix. Surrounded by foliage plants with dramatic leaves – spiky irises, lacy ferns, solid hostas – the smooth simple lines of the terracotta pot look very stylish indeed.

In our Square garden we created another very simple water feature – a half barrel sunk into the ground and planted up with a few small pond plants. Any half barrel in reasonable condition will do, though go for the largest you can find. Most barrels are fine as they are – as the wood gets wet it swells up to close any gaps. If you do seal it with a bitumistic paint, you must let it dry out thoroughly before you fill it with water or else you'll get an oily residue on the surface and the plants won't thrive.

Dig a hole slightly bigger than the barrel, put it in and use a spirit level to make sure it's straight. Since the water line will always be level, it will be very obvious if the barrel isn't in straight and it will irritate you every time you look at it. Pack soil down the sides to hold it in position. Though it may sound daft, when you get to the top, hammer the soil down hard to give you a really firm finish.

As for plants, water lilies (*nymphaea*) are a good choice provided you go for a dwarf variety, and something tall and spiky looks very good breaking the line of the pool. We planted a stripy reed with the off-puttingly long name of *Schoenoplectus lacustris* 'Zebrinus' though it is still often sold under its old name of *scirpus*. In both cases, the plants were growing in soil in special plastic baskets. In the case of the scirpus, it was set on a brick at the bottom of the barrel so it wasn't too deep. The basket also makes a handy stepping stone for any creature that happens to fall in. We didn't put soil into the barrel, figuring that enough would find its way in anyway, as indeed it did. The last step was to add some oxygenating weed, like Canadian pond weed (*Elodea crispa*), to keep the water in the pond healthy.

Think about putting a goldfish or two in your pond as they will eat mosquito larvae. They won't survive the winter outside in such a small volume of water, though, so you'd have to fish them out each autumn and keep them indoors until spring.

Lighting

Lighting in a garden makes an enormous difference to the amount of enjoyment you can get out of it. Not only can you use the garden at night as an outside room, but on long winter evenings you can enjoy looking at it out of the window.

There is plenty of cheap, temporary lighting available – flares, candles, storm lanterns – as well as free-standing solar lights, but in the long run a proper lighting system is best. You can get one installed professionally or, a much cheaper option, install a safe, low-voltage DIY system yourself. All you do is lay the cable around the garden and snap the light fittings onto it wherever you like. There are various styles – tall lanterns, modern-looking tubes or spotlights. The first two are useful for marking a path for example, while spotlights are ideal for highlighting plants and other features.

In the City garden there are two lights shining on the water feature, two fixed to the pergola to light the table and barbecue, and two more at the base of a tree and a shrub. This arrangement is also very effective in winter, illuminating the bare branches and casting interesting shadows on the walls.

> ❛ *Provide several seating areas if you can. After all, the object of the exercise is to enjoy the garden* ❜

Somewhere to sit

To get maximum enjoyment from your garden you need places to sit to make the most of the sun and to get the best views. A seating area or even just a bench can also be an attractive focal point. In our City garden, we put up a simple, triangular wooden pergola in the south-west facing corner to create a sense of privacy since, like most city gardens, it is overlooked by taller buildings. With the table and chairs beneath it, it makes an outside dining room. It's also the perfect opportunity to grow climbing plants.

In the Square garden we sited a simple wooden bench in the sunniest spot and built a metal rose arch over it. Made from black nylon-coated metal, these come in kit form and can be assembled with the minimum of cursing. The arch we chose has panels of lattice infill up the sides, which not only looks good but provides useful support for plants that scramble. To create the feeling of an arbour, you can make a back using hoops and leg extensions from the same range.

Making do

Don't forget that you may already have some features in the garden that can be given a new lease of life. The shed in our Oblong garden is a case in point. Looking more like a beach hut or small summer house than a bog-standard shed, it was wasted where it stood because what you saw from the house was the plain side rather than its more attractive front. With the help of a couple of strong friends it was moved further into the garden and swung round to show the front. The final step was to stain it a lovely subtle moss green from a range of Scandinavian wood stains now available. For the price of a couple of cans of stain, we had a striking new feature and a perfect focal point for the new, sweeping shape of the lawn.

Above: The combination of light and water in our City garden creates a stunning effect at night and using low-voltage, DIY systems for the pump and the lighting make it very quick and easy to achieve. The trellis panels, although functional supports for climbers, are also decorative and the fact that they are raised off the wall on battens means that you get an extremely attractive effect with the shadows.

Right: When fitting the reservoir for the water feature, firm the soil around it to hold it steady.

Left: A barrel pond couldn't be simpler to make. In fact the hardest part is digging the hole deep enough to contain it. It is worth making sure you get it level because if you don't, you will constantly be reminded of the fact by the difference between the waterline and the rim of the barrel.

Below: Choose dwarf varieties of plants that aren't going to take over completely. From an aesthetic point of view, it's a good idea to plant something tall that breaks the line of the rim like this striped rush. Don't forget to add some oxygenating weed to help keep the water clear and healthy.

Everyone, but everyone, has problems of some kind in their garden at some time. Adam and Eve certainly did, though as I recall their pest was just one rather large and articulate snake.

As with so many problems, the best approach is always prevention rather than cure, and there's no doubt that plants that are well grown and well fed and watered are less susceptible to pests and diseases than those that aren't. It's also worth making the effort when buying plants to choose ones that are resistant to disease. Some roses, for example, are specially bred to be resistant to blackspot, while some modern varieties of Michaelmas daisies (*Aster novae-belgii*) are now far less prone to mildew than the older ones.

You need to decide fairly early on whether you want to take an organic approach to gardening or whether you are happy to use pesticides and other chemicals. And it has to be a straight choice because it's very hard to be a 'bit organic'. If you aim not to use chemicals but decide, for example, to spray against greenfly, even if you don't harm any of the insects like ladybirds and lacewings that eat aphids and their larvae, you are still destroying their food source so if they do come to the garden they won't stay and there will be nothing to prevent further infestations of greenfly.

If you do decide to spray, choose a product specifically designed to kill aphids but to leave beneficial visitors like ladybirds, lacewings and hoverflies unharmed. Early morning or late evening are the best times to spray because there are fewer of the beneficial insects around then. If you spray edible crops such as vegetables, be sure that you read the label carefully and don't eat anything until it's safe to do so.

Whichever approach you adopt, though, prompt action is the key. Once a pest has got established on a plant, it does a lot of damage, weakening the plant and making it more likely to get diseases. It is also much harder to get rid of.

Get into the habit of wandering round the garden every day and looking closely at your plants. Apart from anything else it's very pleasurable and there's nothing in the book that says you can't do it with a glass of wine in your hand!

Greenfly and blackfly

These aphids attack a wide range of plants, sucking the sap, weakening the plant and allowing in various diseases. Roses are particularly, but not exclusively, vulnerable to greenfly. Blackfly are partial to the tender growing tips of plants such as broad beans and can distort them horribly.

ORGANIC CONTROL: Wash or rub them off and wait for the ladybirds!

CHEMICAL CONTROL: Spray with an insect-friendly spray or with a systemic one that is absorbed by the plant and poisons the sap, which the aphids suck, for several weeks afterwards.

Slugs and snails

These eat young plants and turn fleshy leaves, like hostas, to lace. In dry weather they hide in moist places under stones or vegetation and come out, ravenous, once it has rained. Eliminating hiding places is one way of keeping down the population.

ORGANIC CONTROL: Encourage frogs and toads, which eat slugs, by building a pond, or tempt hedgehogs into the garden. Contrary to popular belief, hedgehogs are not mad about bread and milk. Cat food is a better bet, though if you feed them too well, they won't want to eat your slugs. Make a barrier around susceptible plants – cut rings from plastic bottles and push them into the soil or scatter a layer of something very sharp on the soil – ashes, baked egg shells, grit, even cocoa shells. If you grow hostas in pots, a band of vaseline round the rim stops those pests climbing up. Digging over the soil in winter, exposing dormant slugs or slug and snail eggs to the frost, also helps.

CHEMICAL CONTROL: Water in a slug-killing chemical or use slug pellets very sparingly – place them individually about 15cm (6in) apart. Not only are they more effective against the pest, but if they are eaten by a pet or a child, a single pellet will do far less harm than a small heap. If you do have small children or pets, a liquid slug killer is the safer option. Don't forget that salt sprinkled onto slugs and snails kills them very effectively. You may think you couldn't possibly kill anything, but once you've seen a much-loved plant destroyed, you'll find any squeamishness rapidly disappears.

Vine weevil

Although the adult beetles can make a real mess of the leaves of shrubs like rhododendrons, it's the grubs that do the most damage. They eat the roots of almost any plant, indoors or out, and often the first clue you get to their presence is plants collapsing and dying for no apparent reason. When you investigate, you won't even have to dig the plants up because they have no roots left to anchor them in the soil.

ORGANIC CONTROL: You can now buy microscopic, parasitic nematode worms which you water into the soil and which destroy the grubs. There is no chemical control.

Flea beetle

These tiny, glossy black beetles, which jump in the air when disturbed, attack members of the cabbage family, wallflowers (*cheiranthus*) and nasturtiums (*tropaeolum*), making masses of pinholes in the leaves. They destroyed a large clump of nasturtiums in our Oblong garden.

ORGANIC CONTROL: Smear a small piece of wood or hardboard with grease and run it across the top of the plants – as the flea beetles jump, they stick to the grease.

CHEMICAL CONTROL: Spray with derris at the first sign of an attack.

Leaf hoppers

These small white creatures, which also jump when disturbed, attack both indoor and outdoor plants, causing an ugly mottling of the leaves. They attacked the purple sage in our Square garden.

ORGANIC CONTROL: Use the greasy board as for flea beetle.

CHEMICAL CONTROL: Either spray with permethrin or pyrethrum. For indoor plants or for a small area in the garden, try plant pins – small cardboard strips impregnated with insecticide – pushed into the soil.

Caterpillars

There are different kinds of caterpillars which attack different plants, doing terrible damage to the leaves, even defoliating a shrub or tree completely.

ORGANIC CONTROL: Pick them off by hand, drown them and leave them for the birds. Think of it as helping the food chain along.

CHEMICAL CONTROL: Spray with derris or with permethrin.

Cats

These are certainly one of the most intractable problems of urban gardening and few things get the red mist rising more than the sight of a large cat using your carefully prepared soil as a litter tray, usually looking you straight in the eye as it does so. There are various products on the market – dust, liquid, gel – which are all supposed to deter cats, but in my experience, none of them work for very long. Some people favour the conditioned reflex approach – blasting them with a hose whenever they appear so they eventually get the message. But even if that works, there are always plenty of new, unconditioned cats to take their place. In our Square garden, we tried a new device – an electronic cat scarer, approved by the RSPCA. When a passing cat breaks the beam it emits a very high-pitched noise which only cats can hear. They dislike it so much they leave. It's always hard to prove a negative, but while Stuart and Mal didn't see any cats bolting from their garden, they didn't see many cats at all, and certainly there was no evidence left in the borders or on the gravel.

Blackspot

These unsightly black blotches affect the leaves of roses and other plants, eventually causing the leaf to turn yellow and die. A bad attack can strip a rose bush of every one of its leaves.

ORGANIC CONTROL: Pick the leaves off as soon as you see any spots and burn them. Choose varieties of roses that are resistant.

CHEMICAL CONTROL: Remove affected leaves, and spray with a copper fungicide at the first sign of trouble.

Powdery mildew

This white felty covering, which affects a whole range of trees, shrubs and perennials, is much worse when the soil is very dry.

ORGANIC CONTROL: Remove and destroy any affected shoots, buds or fruits immediately. Choose mildew-resistant varieties in future.

CHEMICAL CONTROL: Spray with a fungicide when it first appears and at two-week intervals after that. If you find mildew recurring, try a different chemical. Some strains of mildew become resistant to particular fungicides.

Clematis wilt

This disease kills off some or all of the top growth of a seemingly healthy plant. It doesn't go below soil level, though, so that's why you should plant your clematis 10–15cm (4–6in) deeper than they are in their pots so that buds below soil level can produce new growth. There is no organic control, and while you can drench any remaining growth and the soil with fungicide, there is no longer one on the market recommended for this purpose. Smaller-flowered species of clematis are far less susceptible than the larger-flowered varieties.

Left: To keep your plants looking as healthy as this blue Campanula persicifolia *'Telham Beauty', feed and water them well, and look at them every day so that you can nip any problems in the bud.*

We lost four clematises in our gardens during the first summer, some after they had flowered magnificently. It could have been wilt, but since all were planted correctly and none had produced new shoots by the end of the summer, I suspect not. Although they were well watered and their roots protected from the sun, it's likely that weeks of exceptionally high temperatures were more than the young plants could stand.

Weeds

Why the word 'weedy' means weak and pathetic, I'll never know, since weeds are often the most vigorous plants in the garden! Annual weeds aren't a problem. If you mulch the soil well, you won't get many, and you can remove those with a hoe or fork. Perennial weeds like ground elder, bindweed or Japanese knotweed can be a nightmare.

ORGANIC CONTROL: Kill them by depriving them of light. Cover them with old carpet or heavy duty black polythene for a season.

CHEMICAL CONTROL: Use a glyphosate weed-killer which is absorbed right down into the root of the weed. Some of the more persistent weeds will need to be treated more than once.

KILLING BINDWEED

Where bindweed is growing through a shrub, train all the growths you can find up a bamboo cane.

Put a cotton glove over a rubber one and soak it in diluted glyphosate weedkiller. Rub the glove on the bindweed.

The bindweed should die within two to three weeks. If it does not, then repeat the process.

ACKNOWLEDGEMENTS

Grateful thanks are due to the following people:

Jean Bishop for designing the Square garden; Jean Goldberry for the City garden; Robin Williams for the Oblong garden. Michael Twite Landscapes (01789 470505), and Feather & Robinson (0113 282 1077) for construction work. Louise and Learie Hampden for working with us in the gardens.

MATERIALS
Ring the telephone number given for your nearest stockist.
Marshalls of Halifax (01422 366666) for paving in the Oblong and Square gardens; Town & Country Paving (01903 776297) for the paving in the City garden; Harcros Building Supplies (200 branches in the UK); Azco Nobel (01235 862226) for Sadolin Classic wood stain in 'Lupine'; Woodex (01895 234899) for wood stains OS COLOUR Lichen Supra and White Spruce.

ACCESSORIES
Agriframes (01342 328644) for the rose arch; Forest Fencing (01886 812451) for the bench; S & B Evans (0171 729 6635) for the ceramic wall mask; Sankey & Co (0115 927 7335) for the Terraperma pots; Farmer Foster (c/o Hilliers 01794 368944) for the wooden sandpit; Hozelock (01844 291881) for lighting, pond and watering accessories; TDP Ltd (01332 8426685) for garden fleece; Wessex Horticultural Products (01722 742500) for coir hanging basket liners; Concept Research (01763 287764) for the cat scarer; Sherston Earl Vineyards (01666 837979) for the half barrel; The Pier (0171 637 7001) for lanterns and garden candles.

TOOLS
Wilkinson Sword and Spear & Jackson for garden tools; Gardena for tools and watering equipment; Black & Decker (01753 500661) and Qualcast (01449 612183) for lawn mowers.

PLANTS
Bob Collett of Petersham Nurseries (0181 940 5230) for growing all our annuals; Dobies (01803 616281) for begonia tubers; the International Flower Bulb Centre for spring bulbs; Dobies (as above), Mr Fothergill (01638 751161), Suttons (01803 612011) and Thomson & Morgan (01473 688588) for seeds.

FERTILIZERS ETC
Carr's of Weobley (01544 318321) for organic soil improver; Miracle Garden Products (01992 461895) for Osmacote, Miracle Grow and Jumbo Bark Mulch; Sunshine of Africa (01983 754575) for cocoa shells; Rapitest (01490 412804) for soil-testing meter and kits; Levington Horticulture (01473 830492) for autumn lawn food and Slugit; Rooster (01677 422953) for pelleted chicken manure.

Maurice Brown of Marshall's sadly died during the making of the television series. We are all particularly grateful to him for all his help and enthusiasm in the past.

INDEX